Black & White and Read All Over

Also by Arthur Black

Basic Black
Back to Black
That Old Black Magic
Arthur! Arthur!
Black by Popular Demand
Blackmail! (with Lynne Raymond)
Black in the Saddle Again
Black Tie and Tales
Flash Black

Black & White
And Read All Over

ARTHUR BLACK

HARBOUR PUBLISHING

Published by
Harbour Publishing Co. Ltd.
P.O. Box 219
Madeira Park, BC
V0N 2H0
www.harbourpublishing.com

Edited by Susan Mayse
Cover design by Roger Handling
Text design by Mary White
Cover photograph by Howard Fry

Printed and bound in Canada

Harbour Publishing acknowledges financial support from the Government of Canada through the Book Publishing Industry Development Program and the Canada Council for the Arts, and from the Province of British Columbia through the British Columbia Arts Council and the Book Publisher's Tax Credit through the Ministry of Provincial Revenue.

THE CANADA COUNCIL | LE CONSEIL DES ARTS
FOR THE ARTS | DU CANADA
SINCE 1957 | DEPUIS 1957

BRITISH
COLUMBIA
ARTS COUNCIL
Supported by the Province of British Columbia

Library and Archives Canada Cataloguing in Publication

Black, Arthur
    Black & white and read all over / Arthur Black.

ISBN 1-55017-336-7

    1. Canadian wit and humor (English) I. Title. II. Title: Black and white and read all over.

PS8553.L318B48 2004   C818'.5402   C2004-903008-6

Contents

III ||| NATURE BATS LAST

IV ||| RULES OF THUMB

V ||| TEC#NOP#OB!A

I

|||

LIVING DANGEROUSLY

At the Sign of the Red Rooster

I'm not one for name dropping, but I just had breakfast with Jack Nicholson.

Well, sorta. Down at the Red Rooster. You know it? Man, if you have to think about it for even a nanosecond, you've never been there. It's a small restaurant just off the Trans-Canada Highway, roughly halfway between the cities of Victoria and Nanaimo, or halfway between the towns of Duncan and Chemainus, if you want to get nit-picky. Doesn't look like much from the outside, but once you're through the door you're in a whole new world.

Not so much a world as a chicken coop. Oh, the place is clean and bright, with your standard arborite tables and counters, but the décor . . . well, I don't know who owns the joint but whoever it is, they've got a serious case of rooster-philia.

The room is awash with embroidered roosters, sculptured roosters, painted, carved, crocheted and knitted roosters. There are rooster calendars, rooster salt and pepper shakers, the napkin holders are cardboard rooster cutouts and the serviettes come embossed with, but of course, roosters.

I can't speak for the women's facilities but in the men's john I had to conduct my business under the stern beak of a walleyed rooster embroidered on a cloth hanging behind the toilet.

I manfully resisted the urge to ask my waitress the obvious question: why roosters? I figured I'd wait until she told me.

She never did, but she let drop a few other Chicken McNuggets, such as the fact that the Red Rooster's been slinging hash at the same location since 1956, plus the fact that the rooster thing has pretty much gotten out of control.

Customers have caught the disease too. They've brought in rooster memorabilia from pretty well every province and state in North America, not to mention Africa, Portugal, Britain, Holland, Norway, Czechoslovakia, Mexico, Guatemala and Chile.

People have to drive a bit to get to the Red Rooster, but the parking lot always seems to be busy whenever I show up. And a lot of the customers are old-timers. In fact three of the booths have permanent screwed-on signs on them. They read Elmer's Seat, Bert's Seat and Ernie's Seat.

"They're all in their nineties," my waitress explains. "Been coming in here forever."

I think I know why. Having breakfast or lunch at the Red Rooster is the polar opposite of the eating experience you get at a McDonald's, a Harvey's or a Denny's. No antiseptic, one-size-fits-all atmosphere here. The place is folksy and homey and the rooster knickknacks and gewgaws cover the walls and every available space. On your way out, you can buy hot loaves of homemade bread, jars of raspberry jam, or fresh apple and pumpkin pies. The coffee pot is bottomless and they serve up old-fashioned ultra-creamy milkshakes stirred on a whiney old pea-green milkshake machine and served in those battered aluminum jars that I haven't seen since Stompin' Tom was a pup.

You'll need a milkshake and a coffee to wash down the house special, should you order it.

The house special? I was afraid you'd ask. It's Maryland chicken, of course. The menu describes it as breast of chicken with fried banana, gravy, bacon and a corn fritter.

For dessert you get a complimentary card embossed with the emergency hotline number for the Duncan hospital's cardiac unit.

But the Red Rooster doesn't need me to sing its praises. It's already been discovered by Hollywood.

Remember the movie *Five Easy Pieces* with Jack Nicholson? Remember the classic scene where he orders a chicken sandwich that isn't on the menu? And he goes *mano a mano* with the wolverine waitress—and wins?

Well, guess what restaurant that happened at—the Red Rooster! I remember spotting the restaurant sign a couple of decades ago when I first saw the movie.

I asked my waitress if I could sit in the booth where Jack Nicholson sat. She smiled as she topped up my coffee. "Not in this restaurant, honey."

"Whaddya mean," I said. "I saw the Red Rooster sign right up on the screen."

"That's right," said the waitress. "The exterior of the restaurant was in the movie, but for the waitress scene, they used a Denny's down the street."

Too bad for Jack. He doesn't know what he missed.

Accordion Guilt

You know supreme guilt? That stabbing pain that is the physical manifestation of remorse and can make you suddenly wince and knit your brow involuntarily?

All of us have something buried in our past that still has the power to make us jackknife upright in bed at three o'clock in the morning.

Let me tell you about mine.

It's been smouldering on my personal back burner for more than twenty years and I need to get it off my chest. My guilty moment involves a seven-year-old niece . . . and an instrument of torture.

It happened sometime around the end of the seventies in the kitchen of my big sister's house not far from Fergus, Ontario. I was young and much cleverer than I am now—clever to the point of smartassedness, actually. My big sister was both older and more mature. She was also the mother of six. Following a delicious home-cooked meal, she announced that her third youngest, Patti, had an after-dinner surprise for us.

Patti scooted away from the table into a back room and eventually reappeared, harnessed and trussed to a piece of machinery that look like a cross between a portable piano and a smithy's bellows, but made out of Formica.

It was, of course, an accordion. I'd seen them before—even

heard them—but always at a manageable distance. This one was right in my face. Little Patti started to wheeze out "Beer Barrel Polka." I felt a smile taking over the bottom half of my face. She plunged into "I've Got A Lovely Bunch of Coconuts," and my smile turned into a grin, then morphed into a leer.

By the time she was honking out "Lady of Spain," I was cackling uncontrollably, the tears cascading down my cheeks.

It was deeply embarrassing. Little Patti was playing her heart out; others at the dinner table were listening supportively. I was howling like a depraved loon.

I can't help it. Accordions crack me up. I can tolerate bag-pipes. I can keep a straight face through a nose flute recital. But accordions just mess with my mind.

It's hard to say exactly why. Accordions are hardly the apex of earthly annoyance. Not in a world that includes chainsaws, jock-rock DJs and Margaret Atwood reading her own poetry.

And the instrument is not without its champions. The accordion is the official musical instrument of San Francisco, not to mention Detroit, St. Paul and Skokie, Illinois. Gandhi played a version of the accordion, for heaven's sake. So do Laurie Anderson and k.d. lang.

But on the other hand, so do "Weird Al" Yankovic and the Schmenge Brothers.

I think the soaring accordion IQ (irritability quotient) is due to a combination of things. First, there is the music itself, which is invariably schmaltzy and cloying; and then there's the fact that it emanates from such a ludicrous looking contraption—one-third keyboard, one-third aircraft instrument panel, one-third mechanical lung—and all of it covered in a glittery Day-Glo veneer. I've got a hunch Elton John's coffin will look a lot like a top-of-the-line accordion.

And of course it is loud. I am always amazed at the sheer gross volume of—well, noise—that an accordion can pump out.

Sounds like a device that should be outlawed along with mustard gas and anthrax bombs, but the accordion does not terrify people, oddly. It makes them smile, albeit uneasily. Or in my case, guffaw maniacally.

I just hope my niece has kicked her accordion habit once and for all. It's not easy. I know of one hard core accordion player who was heading home after playing at a wedding and decided to stop for a coffee. He pulled in at a roadside diner and went inside. He was just sitting down at the counter when he realized—damn!—he had left his accordion in full view in his car! He rushed back to the parking lot, hoping against hope, but it was already too late.

Someone had smashed in his car window and thrown in two more accordions.

Type L for Lazy

*Work fascinates me. I can sit and look at it for
hours.*

—Anonymous

It's an old bromide but a true one. There is nothing quite as
delicious as having something to do; knowing you have to do
it eventually; realizing that you should get started right now . . .

And then not doing it.

I don't wish to brag, but you are reading the lazily pecked
out words of an expert in idleness. Psychologists divide mankind
into Type A and Type B personalities, Type A being the up-and-
at-'em go-getters who can't sit still and Type B being the more
laid-back, easy-going folks who take life as it comes.

I am Type L for lazy. I'm so laid back that total strangers
come up and take my pulse. Birds check me out as a possible
nesting site. Gangs of kids invite me to join their hockey games.

As a goalpost.

My grade five report card said it all under Teacher's Com-
ments: "Can do better but is lazy."

It's true. That's just the way I am.

And then there's Jean-Dominique Bauby. Mr. Bauby, aged forty-two, was pursuing a very successful career as a journalist—chief editor of *Elle* magazine in Paris—when life threw a little cross-check his way. One minute Bauby was tooling down the highway, driving his son into Paris when he began to feel . . . queer. He pulled to the side of the road and sent his child for help before collapsing in the back seat of his car.

Bauby emerged from a coma three weeks later. Sort of emerged. The new Jean-Dominique Bauby was totally deaf, utterly mute and all but completely paralyzed. So paralyzed that all he could move was his left eyelid.

So it goes. One minute you're a hyper-energetic magazine editor surfing the wave of life; the next you're a helpless, hopeless hospital vegetable. What would you do if you awoke one day to find yourself deaf, speechless and all but totally paralyzed? I'm not sure what I would do, but I know what Jean-Dominique Bauby did.

He wrote a book. A best seller called *Le Scaphandre et le Papillon* (*The Diving Suit and The Butterfly*). It's a fantasy novel about the mental voyages a man embarks on after his body is rendered immobile. Bauby wrote of driving a Maserati down a Formula One racetrack. He imagined what it was like to land as a soldier under withering fire on Normandy Beach on D-Day. He wrote about the haunting, savoury taste of a Lyonnais sausage, the bouquet of a glass of Provençal wine. He wrote about grinding up mountains as a cyclist in the gruelling Tour de France race.

Well, hold on a second, I hear you saying, I thought this guy was paralyzed. How does a deaf-mute quadriplegic write a book, for crying out loud?

No problem for Bauby. He wrote it with the only part of his body he could write with, his left eyelid.

First he invented a simplified alphabet in which the letters were represented by eye-blinks. Then Mr. Bauby dictated—i.e. blinked—the entire 137 page text to an editor friend. They worked at it three hours a day, six days a week, all one summer.

His friends estimate that Mr. Bauby blinked more than 200,000 times to write his novel.

Not content to rest on his laurels, Mr. Bauby turned his attentions to other concerns. He founded an association to help other paralyzed victims and their families. He even started a newsletter for paralytics.

I wish there was a happy ending to this story. I wish I could say that Jean-Dominique Bauby won the Nobel Prize for Literature and that some French medical genius discovered a miracle cure and that Mr. Bauby today can be found behind his chief editor's desk at *Elle*, barking out orders and negotiating with writers and photographers.

But I can't. Life's Department of Dirty Tricks wasn't quite finished with Jean-Dominique Bauby. One week after his novel was published and received wonderful reviews, Mr. Bauby got hit with a second massive stroke and died.

It is tempting to hang one's head and mourn Jean-Dominique Bauby's terrible luck. To rage against the injustice and mutter about the tragedy of it all.

Except it would be wrong. There was nothing tragic about the short, fruitful life of Jean-Dominique Bauby.

He wouldn't permit it.

Don't Fence Me In

It is easy to fly into a passion—anybody can do that—but to be angry with the right person to the right extent at the right time in the right way—that is not easy, and it is not everyone who can do it.

—Aristotle

Ari the Greek knew what he was talking about. I speak as a man who has a crushed computer mouse mounted on his office wall; a near-citation for contempt from a traffic court judge; and a legion of adversaries from my past who would pass on the opportunity to micturate in my ear if my brain was on fire.

I never planned on having a temper. I actually dreamed of becoming one of those suave, laid-back European types, all hooded eyes and Gallic shrugs, devastating my opponents with withering, monosyllabic whispered asides. Instead I matured (I use the word loosely) as a human Krakatoa with a short fuse and a hair-trigger lip. I'd so much rather be Cary Grant.

Or better still, the Fencemaster.

That's not his real name, but that's what he calls himself.

Here is what I know about the Fencemaster: He's a Brit who lives in London, in his late thirties, an office worker who cycles to work each day. That's because he got tired of London's notorious traffic jams, not to mention road rage eruptions and frantic hunts for parking spaces. He discovered, as many urban cyclists have, that pedalling to work each day spared him all that grief and added a patina of serenity to his daily grind.

Thus it was a shock for him to dismount one day in front of the iron fence to which he customarily chained his bike and be confronted by a sign that read: "Howard De Walden Estates Limited. Bicycles found parked against or chained to these railings will be removed without further notice."

It is important to know three things here. First, the De Walden family is one of the UK's wealthiest landowners. Second, the fence in question is in front of a blank building wall. Third, the message was clearly aimed at our hero; he was the only person who ever chained his bike to the fence.

Our hero was surprised, then miffed. Here he was, braving the elements on a bicycle to make his city of 8.5 million citizens somewhat less car-clogged and air-polluted, being told to move on like some kind of vagrant. The smouldering resentment turned to outrage, but quiet outrage, quintessentially British outrage. He dutifully chained his bike elsewhere, muttering to himself, "Bicycles will be removed, eh? Nothing about oh, say, kettles . . . "

He went home, calmly drilled two holes in the bottom of a tea kettle, brought it to work next day and padlocked it to the fence.

The kettle on the fence—surprise, surprise—attracted the attention of passers-by. Tourists started to have their pictures taken standing next to it. The Fencemaster wasn't through. Next he attached a steam iron. Then a refrigerator door. Pretty soon other folks got into the act. An ironing board was chained to the fence. A Georgia licence plate. Stuffed animals. Champagne flutes.

To say that the Fencemaster has caught the imagination of little people everywhere would be an understatement. The fence in question now can barely be seen for all the objects that are attached to it. The Fencemaster has set up a website at www. whatshouldiputonthefence.com. At last count more than three million people had visited the site.

The landlords, who must wish they'd never put up that sign, have sicced the police on the Fencemaster. He came home one day to find three massive bobbies on his doorstep waiting to have a word with him. They turned out to be fans of the website. They suggested that "it might be a good idea not to attach things to the fence any more," but added, "We realize of course you can't stop *other* people from attaching things to the fence."

The Fencemaster can't be certain, but he thinks the bobbies winked.

It's a Crime

*I have never seen a situation so dismal that a
policeman couldn't make it worse.*

—Brendan Behan

Ah, the poor old fuzz. They can't win for losing. Here you
have a group of men and women willing to put their lives
on the line for a fairly paltry paycheque, and what do they get?
Sneers. Jibes. Put-downs.

There's a story going around about a guy who witnesses a
brute of a thug putting the boots to his (the thug's) wife. So the
guy phones the police station, only to be told by an answering
service that "no officer is available to take your call, but if you'll
leave your name and number, the first available agent will get
back to you."

Hell with that, thinks the guy who hangs up and—inspira-
tionally—calls the local Dunkin' Donuts outlet. "Let me speak
to a police officer, please," he tells the server droid who answers.
Within seconds a cop is on the phone, and a squad car is dis-
patched to the scene of the crime.

Great story—but bogus. It's an urban legend, one of those stories that's so good it ought to be true, but isn't.

The fact is that we the public are predisposed to snicker at cops. It helps us to feel superior. Cops, after all, are the folks who can flag us down on the highway, stop us in the shopping mall or pretty much pull us up anywhere they like and lecture us for misbehaviour like no one has lectured us since we were in knee pants in front of our mothers.

Which helps to explain the public glee that greeted a story that appeared in newspapers around the world:

New London, Conn.: A city that doesn't want police officers with "too high an IQ" has been sued by an applicant who lost a job because of his high score on an intelligence test. Robert Jordan claims the city of New London, Connecticut, discriminated against him based on his intelligence and violated his constitutional rights. He says an assistant manager told him, "We don't like to hire people that have too high an IQ to be cops in this city."

"I know I would be a good cop," says Jordan, "but I had the misfortune of selecting too many correct answers."

A would-be cop who was too smart to be a cop. Perfect. Fits right into the urban legend.

Why is it we the public—we fat burghers who take it for granted that the cops will always be there to do our dirty work—feel such delight when we read stories like the foregoing?

Or the following:

An old lady is driving along the highway, steering with her elbows as she knits away. She is swerving all over the road. A highway patrolman draws alongside and shouts through the bullhorn

"*Pull over!*"

The little old lady looks up smiling and says, "No, it's socks, actually."

But cops aren't always the brunt of the joke. There was another story in the paper about a British Columbia motorist who was nabbed in an automated speed trap that measured his speed by radar and photographed his car. He was notified by mail, receiving a photo of his car and a ticket for one hundred dollars.

Being a lawyer and therefore an exceedingly clever fellow, he sent the police department a photograph of a hundred-dollar bill.

Several days later, he received another letter from the police department.

It contained another photograph. Of a pair of handcuffs.

Anchors Aweigh!

You need to be really careful about which words you allow to come out of your mouth—or your word processor. You might find yourself eating them one day.

A few weeks back I am in one of my favourite watering holes nursing a liquid libation when I notice a chap—a stranger—at another table, looking at me.

Not kindly.

I look away, being a polite Canuck, give it a five-beat and look back.

He's still staring at me.

In another lifetime, say ten years ago, I would have zoned into my Clint-Eastwood-High-Noon-eyelock-staredown-what-are-you-lookin-at-bub mode, but life's too short. I consign the voyeur to Anonymous Kookdom, take another sip and—oh, cripes. He's getting up and coming over to my table.

Let's see now. Who do I owe money? Did I ding anyone's car lately? Whose girlfriend might I have innocently ogled? Now he's standing over me. And he's . . . large.

"Yer the guy that writes in the paper arncha?" I nod. It's not really a question.

"And last month you wrote about how much you hate ocean cruises." I nod again. I had written that I thought most ocean cruises were ridiculously expensive and plastic and silly and that a honeymoon on an ocean liner must be, to paraphrase Oscar Wilde, a young bride's second greatest disappointment.

"Yeah," growls the stranger at my table. "Well, I want you to know that I was a cabin steward for four summers on cruise ships out of Miami."

Oh, oh. Reflexively I draw on my martial arts training, surreptitiously tensing my muscles, ready to swiftly morph into an effectively devastating defence posture.

Grovelling, wringing my hands, begging for mercy—whatever it takes.

"And I just want you to know," continues the stranger—Lord, his hands are big!—"that it's way worse than you wrote."

The gist of his beef is that I didn't talk about ocean cruises from the point of view of the poor saps who have to work on them. The pay, he tells me, is crummy. The hours are insane, the accommodations Dickensian and the passengers . . .

Oh, my. The passengers.

The stranger, whose name turns out to be Corey, has a theory about ocean cruise passengers. He figures each and every one of them has a mandatory lobotomy before they come aboard. How else to explain the stupid questions?

Such as the woman sitting poolside one afternoon who asked the cruise director whether the ship's pool was filled with fresh water or sea water.

"Sea water, ma'am," said the director.

"Ah," replied the woman. "That explains why it's so rough today."

Or the passenger who changed his mind about his accommodation once he was aboard. The ship's purser asked him, "Would you prefer an inside cabin or an outside cabin, sir?"

The man squinted his eyes and looked up at the sky. "Better make it an inside cabin. Looks like it could rain."

Or the newlywed couple who had just come aboard. After viewing their cabin, they came storming up to their cabin steward. The bride was crying. The groom was seriously cheesed off.

"You incompetent boobs!" yelled the groom. "We paid for a cabin with a view! And we look out the porthole and what do we see? A parking lot!"

And then there was the passenger—a dentist from Wyoming—who plied Corey with all kinds of inane technical questions, ending with, "Well, tell me, son, does the ship run off generators?"

Corey looked at the man and dead-panned, "Actually, no. We have this very long power cord running to the mainland."

Corey takes a sip of the beer I bought him.

"That happened on my last trip," he recalls.

He's smiling at the memory.

Murphy's Law of Drug Demons

"**A**nything that can go wrong, will."

Murphy's Law, right? Wrong. Everybody thinks that's Murphy's Law but it isn't. It's Finagle's Law. Murphy's Law, first promulgated by a US Air Force engineer in 1949, states, "If there are two or more ways of doing something, and one of those ways can result in a catastrophe, then someone will do it."

The fact that Finagle's Law has been swallowed up and re-christened Murphy's Law is a priceless demonstration of Murphy's Law in action.

The original Murphy's Law has spawned a litter of mongrel offspring. There's Murphy's Corollary, which states, "Left to themselves, things tend to go from bad to worse."

And Murphy's Constant: "Matter will be damaged in direct proportion to its value."

Not to forget the Quantized Revision of Murphy's Law: "Everything will go wrong all at once."

Well, I hate to make the Murphy waters any muddier, but I'm here to tell you that there was a Canadian Murphy's Law long before the US Air Force version. And our version was a helluva lot more powerful. As a matter of fact, thanks to our Murphy's Law, thousands of people in Canada have criminal records they otherwise wouldn't have.

And they owe it all to Emily F. Murphy of Edmonton, Alberta.

Back in the 1920s, Mrs. Murphy was a juvenile court judge and a scribbler of sorts, penning several articles for *Maclean's* magazine.

She was also an idiot, a flaming racist and a zealot slightly to the right of Attila the Hun.

Emily Murphy's pet bugaboo was the demon drug marijuana. She wrote about it under the pen name Janey Canuck. Some of her pearls of wisdom included the observation that marijuana users were "non-white and non-Christian, wanting only to seduce white women."

"Behind these dregs of humanity," thundered Mrs. Murphy, "is an international conspiracy of yellow and black drug pushers whose ultimate goal is the domination of the bright-browed races of the world."

Guess which side of the hash pipe Mrs. Murphy lined up on.

The scary thing about Mrs. Murphy—aside from the fact that she somehow managed to infiltrate the top floor of the Canadian justice system—is that nobody dismissed her for the raving lunatic she was. On the contrary, *Maclean's* eagerly published her frothings. She got a publishing contract and put out a best-selling book about marijuana.

And because of Mrs. Murphy, marijuana got demonized. A relatively harmless barnyard weed metamorphosed into the Demon Drug. A fiendish fix which, Mrs. Murphy assured her readers, "has the effect of driving [smokers] completely insane. The addicts lose all sense of moral responsibility and are immune to pain . . . become raving maniacs, liable to kill or indulge in any form of violence using the most savage cruelty."

A gullible Canadian public—and government—bought every word. Mrs. Murphy's incendiary ravings were the signal reason marijuana was declared illegal in Canada.

"A decision was made without any scientific basis, nor even

any real sense of social urgency, placing cannabis on the same basis as the opiate narcotics, and it has remained so to this day."

My words? Nope. That's a quote from Justice Gerald LeDain's Royal Commission report of 1972.

Let me leave you with another quote. This one comes from Charlie Mackenzie, retired but not forgotten leader of the regrettably dormant Canadian Rhinoceros Party and the chap from whom I poached the story of Emily Murphy. Charlie sez we should look at it this way:

"In 1923, marijuana smoking was relatively unknown in Canada . . . no one outside of a few jazz musicians used it to get stoned. Today, according to the RCMP, five million Canadians use it for no other purpose.

"If no one smoked it in 1923 when it was legal, and five million smoke it today when it's not, something's gone wrong. Ergo, Murphy's Law."

Now that just breaks me up, but somehow I don't think Mrs. Murphy would be amused.

Loaded for Bear

Life has a funny way of getting your attention. For Isaac Newton, it was an apple on the noggin. For Archimedes, it was noticing how the water level rose when he got into the bathtub.

For Troy Hurtubise, it was getting knocked flat by a grizzly bear he calls the Old Man.

It happened on the banks of Humidity Creek in northern British Columbia back in 1984. Hurtubise was by himself, panning for gold along a creek, when he looked up and saw, staring back at him, a grizzly big enough to block out the sun.

The bear was so big and so powerful that it sent Hurtubise sprawling with a blow from its *snout*. Hurtubise was reasonably certain that he was living through his last few moments on earth, but the bear, unaccountably, lost interest and strolled off into the bush.

Needless to say, Hurtubise would never forget the encounter, but what really rattled him was the feeling of absolute helplessness that washed over him when he faced that bear. He couldn't run, he couldn't hide, and the idea of fighting back was utterly ludicrous.

Personally I am quite comfortable with the knowledge that even a puny grizzly could kick my butt in a nanosecond, but not Troy Hurtubise. He resolved that day to figure out a way that he could stand up, unarmed, in front of a wild grizzly and live to tell about it.

Thus began Project Grizzly, one man's personal quest to create a grizzly-proof suit. Hurtubise retired to his basement workshop and went to work. Using only basic tools and a welding torch he's worked his way through several prototypes—from early models incorporating not much more than hockey equipment and duct tape to Robocop-like suits of armour made from heavy-gauge aluminum, stainless steel, high-tech plastic, titanium—you name it.

And he's built some pretty tough suits. Suits that could withstand a blast from a 12-gauge shotgun at six metres, a fifty-metre drop off the Niagara Escarpment, eighteen different encounters with a three-tonne pickup going fifty kilometres an hour and assault by a 160kg log swinging down from ten metres up in a tree. The suits survived and so did Hurtubise, who was inside them.

His latest model—he calls it the Ursus Mark VII—is more like a lunar landing craft than a body suit. It contains an air-conditioning unit, protective airbags, robotic hands (Hurtubise manipulates them with his tongue), a built-in computer and a video screen which allows the wearer to have 360-degree vision without moving his head.

Hurtubise, who must strip to his shorts and cover his body with Vaseline just to get into the Ursus Mark VII, figures he's put more than sixteen hundred hours and over $200,000 into this model alone.

That's enough to earn him a spot in the *Guinness Book of World Records* for having the world's most expensive research suit, but it still doesn't answer the only question that really matters to Troy Hurtubise: is Ursus Mark VII tough enough to withstand an all-out attack from an enraged bear?

That's Hurtubise's big problem right now—he can't find a suitable dancing partner. Pickup trucks, swinging logs, even a gang of toughs with baseball bats and crowbars are old hat now. He wants to meet a bear. The thing is, bears in captivity don't have the untamed edge that makes a grizzly in the wild such an awesome force of nature.

But wild grizzlies are hard to find. Especially if you're clomping around in a high-tech suit of armour.

Still, should you happen to find yourself on the banks of Humidity Creek sometime and you spot a critter than looks like a cross between the Michelin Man and a Marvel Comics action figure, pay it no mind.

That's just Troy Hurtubise looking for a rematch.

Manners Maketh Man

"If niceness were an Olympic sport, Canadians would be perennial champions, like Kenyans in the marathon."

—Robert Fulford

It's true: Canadians—providing you don't count hockey arenas and Normandy beaches—are just about the meekest folks on the planet. If you don't believe that, just ask one of us. In fact one of the easiest ways to tell a Canadian from an American is to step on his toe. If the guy tells you that *he's* sorry, you've just trod on a Canadian.

Americans, of course are world-renowned for their, well, they would call it frankness. The rest of the world views it as rudeness. The Ugly American is not just an old movie title. It's a sociological cliché recognized from Copenhagen to Canberra.

Not to mention from Seattle to Sarasota. Even Americans acknowledge that they're rude and getting ruder. A recent national survey by a research group called Public Agenda showed that seventy-nine percent of Americans polled believe a lack of courtesy and respect in that country is a serious problem. Sixty-one percent of them believe the problem has worsened in recent years.

Well, maybe. But politeness can be overdone too. Take the situation in Japan, where one of the fastest growing niche industries is a service called *wakaresaseya*. That translates literally as "breaker-upper"—and that's just what these folks do—they break up sticky relationships. A *wakaresaseya* company employs agents who, for a price, will dump your girlfriend, get rid of your husband or fire that longtime employee for you.

Why can't the Japanese individuals do their own dirty work? Because in Japanese culture, politeness is paramount. The Japanese find it exceedingly difficult to just say "no." Far easier to hire a *wakaresaseya* hitman (or woman) to do the job for a fee.

In Korea the problem isn't getting out of unwanted relationships, it's getting into wanted ones. It is an unwritten but universally observed rule of public behaviour in South Korean society to shun voluntary contact with strangers. It's a tenet of decorum that makes for a lot of lonely Saturday nights, but it helps explain why in Seoul there are currently eight "booking clubs" in which single men and women pay waiters to forcibly introduce them to each other. For a few hundred bucks, a waiter will take the client by the elbow and physically steer him or her to the table of their choice, then do the honours. "Kim, this is Lee. Lee, meet Kim. Now what'll yez have?"

There's turmoil in Thailand over politeness too. The Thais place a high premium on civil behaviour and public harmony. Right now that's being shredded by probably the most ill-mannered electronic export the West has ever foisted on the rest of the world: the TV show called *The Weakest Link*, wherein a sadistic and overbearing hostess browbeats and humiliates contestants who fail to answer questions correctly.

There are versions of *The Weakest Link* playing in seventy different countries, mostly to enthusiastic audiences. Not so in Thailand. The Thai version of the show has shocked the populace and provoked a huge uproar. Why? Because it's too rude.

The government-sponsored National Youth Bureau went so

far as to write an official letter of protest to the company that produces the show complaining that "the show is promoting fierce competition and selfishness among participants. This contravenes Thai generosity."

Even Prime Minister Thaksin Shinawatra was moved to comment, "I felt rather stressed out after watching the show."

Somehow I don't think Thailand is ready for *Coach's Corner* with Don Cherry.

Ah, well, rudeness wasn't invented yesterday. And it doesn't just thrive in TV studios or New York taxis. Human beings have always been convinced that civilized behaviour was going to hell in a handbasket, and we've usually placed the blame squarely on the shoulders of the next generation.

Like the grump who said, "The children now love luxury. They have bad manners, contempt for authority; they show disrespect for their elders and love chatter in place of exercise. They no longer rise when elders enter the room. They contradict their parents, chatter before company, gobble up dainties at the table, cross their legs, and tyrannize over their teachers."

Who said that—Ann Landers? Stockwell Day? A *Globe and Mail* editorial?

Nope. Socrates. About twenty-five hundred years ago.

But Is It Art?

Does anybody remember what art is? I knew once, many years ago. I was standing in a cave near a town called Altamira in northern Spain. For a few *pesetas*, a local guide had agreed to escort a half dozen of us into an already famous underground grotto decorated with prehistoric paintings. The beam of his flashlight flickered across the cave wall revealing depictions of deer, bison, a few hand prints—and then the guide flicked off the flashlight, leaving us in complete darkness.

After a few seconds he struck a kitchen match and as it flared, he held it close to one of the painted bison.

The bison breathed.

In the dancing flame of the match, the bison seemed to come alive. A few of us actually jumped.

The painting was fifteen thousand years old, put there by a half-naked, illiterate savage who never saw a paint brush, much less a copy of *Gray's Anatomy*, but I did not doubt for a second that it was art. It went straight from the cave wall through my eyes to my heart.

I've never been that sure of a piece of artwork since.

I remember standing in an art gallery in Toronto in front of a metre-and-a-half section of sewer pipe. It was entitled "This is Not a Sewer Pipe" and carried a price tag of five hundred dollars.

One of Canada's most famous living artists is Jana Sterbak. Famous for what? For "Vanitas: Flesh Dress for an Albino Anorectic." It's a sculpture consisting of rib-eye steaks sewn together and left to rot in public.

And I mean public. It was shown at the National Gallery of Canada in 1989.

Or consider the opus of New Yorker David Leslie. Mr. Leslie is a performance artist who thinks "the world needs art that breaks conventions of beauty." That's why his latest artistic statement will take place in a boxing ring. The artist plans to don boxing gloves and protective head gear, then invite anyone in the audience to come into the ring and try to knock him out.

"I'll be covering up," he said, "but people will have, like, fifteen uninterrupted shots at me. It'll be cool."

Then there's the photographic artist Thomas Condon in Cincinnati. He tried to have an art opening consisting of photographs he'd taken in a morgue. Condon had arranged various corpses so that they were holding objects like a syringe, sheet music and an apple. Cincinnati police reckoned it was more like corpse abuse than art, and Condon's been indicted—although a local art critic allowed that "from an art perspective, there is a precedent for [such an exhibit]."

Perhaps the "What is art?" question came full circle at an exhibit in Birmingham, England, recently. The exhibit consisted of . . . nothing. There were no sculptures on the floor, no paintings on display, only stark white walls and a few cardboard signs that read, "Exhibition to Be Constructed in Your Head." An organizer explained that it was "an experiment to see how people react to it."

They want to be careful about encouraging public judgment. They should bear in mind what happened at an avant-garde space called the Eyestorm Gallery in London's trendy West End. Gallery officials opened their doors the morning after a launch party for artist Damien Hirst, only to discover that one of Mr. Hirst's installations had disappeared! Police questioned a building cleaner, Emmanuel Asare, who readily admitted that when he saw a coffee table littered with cigarette butts, empty beer bottles, pop cans and paper cups, he sighed, swept the whole thing into a garbage bag and tossed it in a dumpster.

When he was informed that he had dismantled a work of art valued at twelve thousand dollars, Asare shrugged and said, "I didn't think for a second that it was a work of art. Didn't look much like art to me."

The world needs more art critics like Emmanuel Asare.

Rich Man, Poor Man

This is a story about two men. One of them is royalty: Prince Jefri of Brunei. The other man is a commoner, a salesman: Joe Segal of Vancouver.

Prince Jefri first. His country, Brunei, is a tiny kidney bean of a nation about the size of Prince Edward Island. It sits like an afterthought on the brow of Borneo and would be a totally forgettable backwater sultanate but for the fact that it is filthy, stinking rich with crude oil.

Prince Jefri—a royal son of Brunei—is, to put it mildly, a conspicuous consumer. He owns two thousand automobiles—personally. He holds the keys to seventeen different aircraft. He has a huge yacht, tastefully named *Tits*, which carries two high-powered Zodiac tenders: *Nipple One* and *Nipple Two*.

Mind you, he doesn't spend all of his time on *Tits*. Sometimes he lives in his palace. The one with 1,778 rooms.

Prince Jefri has other expensive tastes. He sponsors the Ferrari Formula One team on the international racing circuit. He's fond of calling up Miss USAs, Miss Worlds and other planetary sirens of pulchritude and offering them thirty thousand US dollars a week to come and "entertain" him and the boys at the palace.

The prince is a young man. He has four wives, three children, his own private polo team and more mistresses than

Casanova ever dreamed of. But times are hard. Recently he pe-
titioned his brother, the Sultan of Brunei, for $500,000 US to
cover "ordinary living expenses."

That's five hundred grand a month, you understand.

That's Prince Jefri. Then there's Joe Segal.

Like Prince Jefri, Joe is a rich man, but that's where the
similarities end. For starters, Joe earned his dough. Joe was
born not with a silver spoon in his mouth, more like a pick
and shovel in his hands. He started out slinging gravel for the
Alaska Highway project back in the forties. Soon he moved
into sales. Before he was finished—and he's not finished yet—
Joe created Fields Department Stores. And merged it with
Zellers. Which he sold to Hudson's Bay Company. He was
also the man behind Sterling Shoes, First National Properties
and one or two dozen other flourishing concerns. Add it all
up and Joe Segal of Vancouver, like Prince Jefri of Brunei, is
a very rich man.

He also spends lavishly, but not on hookers or Lear jets or
yachts. Joe Segal spends his money on people. He has earned
that most old-fashioned of descriptions: philanthropist.

He has ploughed his dough into universities and colleges in
Canada and Israel. Also children's hospitals, homes for the aged,
the Italo-Canadian Society, the Vancouver Police Foundation,
Crime Stoppers International, the Canadian National Institute
for the Blind.

Has he been recognized and honoured for his generosity?
Oh, sure. Joe's got an Order of British Columbia and an Order of Canada and a drawer full of medals and certificates and
plaques, but he's faintly embarrassed when somebody brings it
up because he doesn't do it for the glory. Joe Segal shares his
wealth for a very selfish reason: because he learned a long time
ago that the very most satisfying thing you can do in life is give
to others.

"Give till it hurts," says Joe, "then give a little more."

Corny? Perhaps. But I can show you two men—one, a Ma-
laysian prince with luxury cars and private jets and yachts, a

palace, a cavalcade of courtesans—even a twelve-million-dollar diamond and ruby encrusted carpet beside his bed . . .

And then I'll show you another man—Joe Segal—with a chequebook full of stubs.

Now you tell me which one is rich and which one is poor.

Take a Flyer

Christmas comes but once a year, and frankly, that's frequently enough for me. And I'm not alone. For some people—many people in fact—this holiday doesn't always play out like a Currier & Ives print or a Disney family special.

For some folks, even when times aren't tough, Christmas is a tough time. The writer Jimmy Cannon says, "Christmas is a holiday that persecutes the lonely, the frayed and the rejected." Even P.G. Wodehouse has his perennially optimistic Bertie Wooster sigh, "We shall soon have Christmas at our throats."

I know what Bertie means. For me this is in some ways a sad and wistful time. At Christmas my thoughts go back to an old friend I haven't seen in years. And I get melancholy at the thought that I will not see him again. I'm talking about Flyer.

There's a kind of backhanded journalistic connection to all this. I have two things in common with newspaper tycoons. Number one, my name is Black, which is thankfully my only connection with Conrad. And number two, like the thinly disguised William Randolph Hearst in Citizen Kane, I miss my sled.

His, according to the movie, was called Rosebud. I never named mine. It had Flyer emblazoned in red paint across the steering bar, and I guess that was name enough for me.

I remember it like a brother: four maple slats rivetted on to a steel skeleton that ended in two thin red runners; the wooden steering bar across the front was tethered by a loop of hemp to tug it up from the bottom of the hills. You could sit up on the Flyer and steer with your feet, but that made it top-heavy and you the butt of derision. Only sucks and little kids sat on their sleds. The proper thing to do was to run at the crest of a hill in a banzai hunch and throw yourself on the sled at the last moment. I still remember the unpredictable spitfire squirtyness of that sled . . . the way it rattled your breastbone as you clattered across icy ruts . . . the way the wind whipped your face as you flew down the hill.

The way you assaulted the hill in run after run, far past the waning of the watery afternoon sun, until your hands were numb and you minced home on frozen feet, trying not to cry and hoping that somebody else would be there to undo your frozen laces.

The sled, on the other hand, was unmoved. It was amazingly invulnerable. Not counting the stout and unbreakable steering bar there were no moving parts, nothing to break down or fall off. Aside from flinging it off a cliff or running over it with a Zamboni there wasn't much you could do to hurt those old-time sleds. They stayed in families for years, like heirlooms, being handed down to younger siblings and eventually handed off to new nephews and nieces.

Not to go all Andy Rooney on you, but you never see a simple sled anymore. Now they have brakes and steering systems and tenders and moveable runners and, I suspect, a lot of breakdowns.

And it doesn't look like its getting better. News item came across my desk yesterday announcing that there's a new sled on the market. Made by . . . Porsche.

That's right. Porsche. It has an aluminum frame, stainless steel runners, weighs five kilos and comes with—get this—a nylon carrying case into which it can be folded for easy carrying back to the top of the slopes.

That isn't sledding. That's commuting.

And it doesn't cost nine ninety-five like my old Flyer. The Porsche sled costs over five hundred dollars.

Cheap enough for the upwardly mobile, I suppose, who can't wait to let it drop in casual conversation that they've got a Porsche in the garage.

My Christmas dream would be to one-up them with a comeback: I'd say, "Really? I have a Flyer."

Button-Down Lemmings

The trouble with unemployment is that the minute you wake up in the morning, you're on the job.

—Slappy White

Ever been fired? I don't mean downsized, dehired, streamlined or any of the other weasel euphemisms currently in vogue. I'm talking about flat-out, in your face, slam-dunk canned. Where somebody with a bigger desk than yours looks you in the eye and tells you, "We don't want you to work here any more."

I have. No one could call it a pleasant experience, getting fired. It's hard on your wallet and on your self-esteem. It's been twenty-five years since my old boss Stricker in the *Globe and Mail* advertising department called me into his office and ominously closed the door behind me. I remember now that everybody in the office was looking studiously down at their desk as I disappeared into the inner sanctum. They already knew what I was about to learn. A quarter of a century and I can still feel the humiliation.

No hard feelings, mind you. Stricker was absolutely right

to fire me. As a newspaper advertising salesman I was a total disaster. Each workday morning I'd exit the *Globe and Mail* office with my fellow salesmen. Like button-down lemmings we'd march out of the office, briefcases at our side to "make calls." Actually, we usually slipped around the corner and into a greasy spoon where we sipped bad coffee and told worse jokes. Then about quarter to ten we'd all straighten our ties, check our shoeshines, grab our briefcases and hit the pavement.

The other guys went off to make their calls just as good salesmen are supposed to. I pretended to be doing the same thing, but after a furtive glance or two, I strolled a few blocks to a poolroom where I shot eight ball until the movie houses opened. Or I went to the YMCA and ran laps on the indoor track. Or checked my briefcase in a bus station locker and wandered around the museum. Anything but sell advertising. I hated selling.

It couldn't go on, of course, and it didn't. After just a few weeks my dismal performance came to the attention of my boss and the rest was history. As was I.

And it's taken twenty-five years for me to realize that getting fired was one of the best things that ever happened to me. Because imagine if I'd turned out to be a hotshot—or even a mediocre—salesman? Chances are I would have stayed in that line of work. Chances are I'd be selling ad space today. And still hating every moment of it.

Besides, it turns out that getting fired can be a good sign. A story in (oh, sweet irony) the *Globe and Mail* notes that some of the great figures in history got the sack on their way up. Albert Einstein was unceremoniously fired as a young man. Thomas Edison was too. Henry Ford got the hook. Even late-night yapper David Letterman and diminutive sex guru-ess Ruth Westheimer each got pink slips before they got famous.

Makes sense when you think about it. You can't put a size-ten foot in a size-eight shoe. People who are unhappy in their work are going to do a lousy job. And bosses are always on the lookout for people doing lousy jobs.

In the selling game, lousy performance shows up pretty

quickly. I also remember now how my colleagues, the other salesmen, lived in dread of "the monthly roundup." That's when Sales Manager Stricker totted up all the advertising space that had been sold, and by whom, and handed out congratulations to the hotshots.

And a private, closed-door, one-on-one "chat" to the also-rans.

Nobody wanted one of those chats. And the fear of them gave rise to a paranoid hatred of Sales Manager Stricker.

I still remember one morning in the coffee shop, six or seven of us sitting around waiting to start the day of "making calls." The talk turned, as it often did, to "what I'll do when I win the lottery."

Ronnie, one of the quieter ones, surprised us all by saying, "The day after I win the lottery, I'm coming down to the office and I'm gonna pee all over Stricker's desk."

Everybody laughed. Everybody except Danny.

"Not me," said Danny. "I plan to hire someone to do it for me."

Another Hat Trick

Let's hear it for the Stetson hat. It's eponymous, you know. Named after its creator, John B. Stetson. With a handle like that you pretty well have to wear a cowboy hat, right? "Name's John B. Stetson, pilgrim." Conjures up an image of a lean and rangy Texan with knobby hands and skin like saddlebag leather.

Actually John B. Stetson was a citizen of New Jersey, and a pretty frail and sickly one at that. A hat maker in Hoboken, back in the mid-1800s, Stetson developed tuberculosis and decided to go west for his health. High in the mountains of Colorado he used his haberdashery expertise to turn a fur pelt into an un-likely looking head covering that protected him from the rain, wind and sun. A passing cowboy took one look at the thing on Stetson's noggin and bought it off him for five dollars cash on the barrel. Stetson knew a good thing when he saw it. He returned back east and went into business in Philadelphia, turning out the wide-brimmed, high-crowned hats that bear his name to this day.

But wearing a Stetson in public anywhere outside Alberta or interior BC is a risky business these days. I blame John Travolta for that. A Stetson used to be the epitome of manliness . . . then Travolta appeared in the movie *Urban Cowboy* . . . wearing one of those particularly dopey-looking Stetsons with the feathers on the front and a big hump in the crown that looks like a breaching whale. Travolta made it okay for goofs to wear Stetsons. And that was the beginning of the end for a great hat, I fear.

Well, not just Stetsons . . . men's hats in general. You hardly ever see men in hats any more. I mean serious hats—Stetsons, fedoras, trilbys or bowlers. And that's a relatively new wrinkle in the fashion parade. Hats have been around for a long time. Just look at how they've infiltrated the language. Hockey players may wear helmets but they still score hat tricks. Politicians throw their hats in the ring at the drop of a hat, when they're not going hat in hand to the electorate. And I'm not talking through my hat here. In fact, if it wasn't kind of old hat, I'd pass the hat round for them. But keep that under your hat.

Then of course there's the phrase that Alice in Wonderland made popular: mad as a hatter. They say mercurous nitrate, a chemical once used in the manufacture of felt hats, was more than toxic enough to poison haberdashers, giving them tremors and spasms. The popular name for the condition was "mad hatter's disease."

Nothing mad about John B. Stetson, the hatter from Hoboken. He parlayed a piece of fur in the Colorado mountains into a multi-million-dollar business and a household name.

Not to mention the canyons of Academia. There's a John B. Stetson Middle School in Pennsylvania and a John B. Stetson University in Florida.

That's a lot of magic to pull out of a hat. Even a Stetson.

The High Cost of Being Famous

"I get between two thousand and five thousand fan letters a month and we answer them all. Being famous runs me to about $25,000 a year in stamps, coloured photos and a secretary to answer it all."

So spake Wayne Gretzky at the height of his hockey celebrity a few years ago. Sounds like a set of problems a lot of us would like to have, but maybe not. Oh, yeah, celebrities get the red carpet treatment—the best tables in restaurants, free limo rides, adoring fans—but there's a downside to being a household name too.

Much of the front page of the *Vancouver Sun* one day recently was taken up by a photo of a pudgy, bespectacled, slightly cranky-looking middle-aged white man with orange hair shuffling down a city street.

The photo was in full colour and splashed across three columns. Must be a pretty significant news story, I thought. A visiting prime minister perhaps? A UN dignitary? A Mafia kingpin on his way to trial?

No, the photo caption reveals that it was only Elton John, the pop singer. And he was shopping in downtown Vancouver.

The news story below the photo emphasized that all the investigative resources of the *Vancouver Sun* were unable to ascertain exactly what Mr. John purchased during his ten-minute downtown walkabout, but that "we do know that he made a purchase, thanks to an alert BC-CTV cameraman, who was able to run from his office and record the star getting into a dark-coloured van. A bodyguard had a bag of purchases."

This nonstory proves the world has finally absorbed and digested the horrors of September 11. We're back to our usual fatuous pursuits, including the cult of celebrity.

Strange phenomenon, celebrity worship. Used to be confined to the high-born, the desperado and the filthy rich. The Brits cut the dotty and dysfunctional Windsors all kinds of slack because they carry "royal" blood in their veins. Common folk revered Robin Hood because he gave handouts to the poor. People deferred to the Morgans and the Rockefellers because they hemorrhaged greenbacks wherever they went.

Today we're less choosy. We make celebrities of potty-mouth rappers, anorexic teenaged clothes horses and two-metres-plus freaks in baggy shorts whose only talent is stuffing a ball through a hoop.

Andy Warhol was wrong. People aren't famous for fifteen minutes; they're famous forever. Somewhat. Adam West was the actor who portrayed Batman on TV a million years ago. He's still out there, in cape and mask, opening shopping malls and making guest appearances at plumbers' conventions. Ozzy Osbourne used to be a rock star. Now, he's a clapped out, drug-addled mumbler with about eleven functioning brain cells, but that's all right—he's a celebrity, so he gets his own TV show.

Celebrities get the trappings, but they also get trapped in a klieg-lit time capsule. Wayne Gretzky is always going to have to talk about hockey. Ozzy Osbourne will always be a petrified rock star. Nobody is ever going to ask Adam West to audition for the part of Hamlet.

Dini Petty is a Canadian who has known the mantle of celebrity. She started off in the media game by hitching a ride in a helicopter to do radio traffic reports over the streets of Toronto and wound up with her own daily TV show. Does she like being famous?

"I don't think fame is worth a tinker's dam because it's very intrusive and the more you have the more intrusive it is. If I had to do it all over again, I'd rather just be rich."

Which takes me back to that newspaper photo I started out talking about, the one of a dyspeptic-looking Elton John walking down a Vancouver street. Only now I'm looking at the photograph from his point of view—a guy who's just trying to go out on a simple shopping expedition—and here's this idiot television cameraman cantering along beside him with a Sony Portacam on his shoulder, grinding away.

He's Elton John. He's got enough money to buy a six-pack of castles in Spain. There's scarcely a door in any city in the world that he wouldn't be welcomed at and fawned over.

But he can't walk down the street and buy a couple of CDs or a pair of socks in peace.

No wonder he looks so cranky.

Taking a Chance on Life

So I'm sitting in my car at the pump while the gas jockey fills my tank with unleaded regular. The ignition is switched off, but I've got the key turned to 'accessories' so I can listen to the radio. The pump jockey leans in my window and says, "I'm afraid I have to ask you to turn your car radio off, sir."

"Why is that?" I ask.

"Risk of a spark, sir. There was a gas station in Alberta that blew up because a customer had his radio on while he was getting gas."

Meekly—I'm Canadian, eh?—I turn my ignition key to 'off.' I pay for the gas and drive away, making sure my wristwatch doesn't accidentally brush against the window crank producing a spark that will turn the entire town into flaming Armageddon.

And then I think . . . wait a minute.

I've been filling up at gas stations at least once a week for the last forty years. Just about everybody I know has been doing the same thing. I can remember seeing guys pumping gas with cigarettes in their mouths. I have never, in four decades, heard of *any* fire caused at a gas pump *anywhere* by a spark from a car ignition.

On the other hand, maybe the kid was right. Perhaps I'm just an aging desperado who's grown used to living dangerously.

By rights I shouldn't even be here. I should have died from extreme carelessness years ago.

When I was growing up, my parents never strapped me into a kiddy's car seat, mainly because there weren't any. In those days, kids got to bounce around in the back seat along with the family mutt. We could even roll the windows down and fall out if we wanted to.

The only air bag I knew was an American Airlines stewardess who lived down the street.

Heck, I was lucky to live that long, really. I spent a lot of my infancy in a non-CSA-approved crib, and I'm pretty sure my blankets weren't treated with flame retardant. I know I spent a lot of lazy afternoons gnawing on the crib rails with my new teeth. Crib rails sporting a bright red coat of lead-based paint.

Amazing I don't glow in the dark.

And diet! Every nickel I could scrape up by cutting lawns (without safety glasses or noise reduction earmuffs) went for Hostess Twinkies, twelve-ounce bottles of Kik Cola and all the bubble gum I could stuff between my jaws.

And if we were really good at home, Mum might make us our favourite between-meals snack, a slice of Christie's white bread: sliced, slathered with butter and then liberally sprinkled with brown sugar. Sometimes on hot days she'd even give us a pitcher of sugar-laced Freshie. Otherwise we'd just drink water from the garden hose.

Medic! We got a dead man walking, here!

As kids we suffered from a dreadful lack of rules and supervision. We had peashooters and homemade bows and arrows. Bike helmets? Closest I got was a Davy Crockett coonskin cap. Dogs ran free. We cooked up our own pickup games of baseball and touch football without a single coach! We played hockey on outdoor rinks without dressing rooms or anyone to help us with our skates. Some of us even got hurt and had to get over it on our own. It was a brutal time.

We spent summer afternoons swinging on a rope tied to a branch of a huge maple tree. You took a mighty sprint, grabbed the rope, soared out over the river, let go of the rope and land-ed in the swimming hole—if you timed it right. If you timed it wrong, you landed in a raspberry patch. There was no lifeguard, the rope was rotten and the branch could have come down at any time.

Mind you, by then we had already been coarsened by years of classroom barbarity. Kids nowadays won't believe this, but in those dark ages, some of us actually *failed our year*. That's right, we were held back and forced to repeat a year's worth of dreary classes until we got it right. It was all based on some primitive academic theory that certain kids were actually smarter or worked harder and therefore deserved preferential treatment. Thank heavens we've stamped out that kind of thinking.

We live in much safer times now, but it can feel a little cramped. A smarter guy than me once said, "A ship is safe in harbour—but that's not what ships are for."

Applies to humans too.

Say Goodnight, Mavis

In tragedy, every moment is eternity. In comedy,
eternity is a moment.

—Christopher Fry

In the early spring of 1996, tragedy fell on sixty-four-year-old
Mavis Pickett like a Mack truckful of boulders. It arrived in
the form of a telephone call from a policeman in Whistler, BC.
Her thirty-year-old daughter, also named Mavis, was dead. She
had tumbled off a cliff while skiing at Blackcomb mountain.

"She was my soulmate," remembers Mavis senior. "We could
finish each other's sentences."

Poised on the cusp of senior citizenry, when life is supposed
to smooth out and become simplified and pleasant, Mavis was
instead plunged into a whirlpool of misery, faced with an un-
thinkable, inconsolable loss. So the grey-haired, bespectacled
grandmother did the only thing she could.

She became a stand-up comic.

Actually it was an accident. Searching for some kind of relief
from her pain, Mavis came across a night school brochure offering a course in grief management through humour. She signed

up. At her first class, her heart fell when she discovered she'd enrolled not in a lecture series, but in a stand-up comedy workshop. Not for me, she thought firmly. She was no stand-up comedian. She was a retired elementary school teacher, for heaven's sake. She tried to withdraw from the course. The teacher sensed something special in Mavis and begged her not to give up just yet, to at least attend a couple of classes and give it a shot.

Turned out Mavis had superb natural timing and a great stage presence. She also had a personal comic motherlode of material all to herself

There's a hoary old adage for writers that advises them to "write about what you know." Mavis decided she would take her humourous material from an area of life that she knew all about, that curiously no other stand-up comedian was tackling: what it's like to get older.

It became an absolute gold mine. Other stand-up comics were screaming and yelling about sex and booze and Osama bin Laden in sulphurous X-rated rants. Mavis toddled out to the microphone and talked in a sweet voice about forgetfulness, decreased agility, fading eyesight and other hurdles of advancing age.

She never swears during her act, but she's not exactly a goody-two-shoes out there on the stage.

"Young people are really concerned about what old people think," she purrs into the microphone. "Just the other day, my granddaughter asked me 'Did you and Grandpa have mutual orgasms?' And I said, well, no dear. We had Metropolitan Life."

It didn't take the world of stand-up long to discover the fresh new voice coming out of Vancouver. Mavis is a smash. She's appearing at night clubs, cafes and conventions all over the city and the lower mainland. She could work just about every night if she wanted to, but she doesn't. She's got a real life. She also teaches osteo-fit classes to fellow seniors six days a week. "That's where I pick up some of my best material," she says.

The best thing about Mavis? Her exit line. Most stand-up comics invariably end their routines with lame and hapless bail-out lines like "Hey, you've been a terrific audience. Thangyuh-verrrymuch."

Not Mavis. When she finishes her last joke, she pauses, beams out at the audience and says quietly "Say goodnight, Mavis." By this time, the audience is in love with the woman. The whole room roars "*Goodnight, Mavis!*" over their own applause.

Except Mavis is not really talking to the audience. She's talking to a specific person she can see sitting and laughing in the front row.

It's Mavis Anne, her daughter. Mavis Pickett is the only one who can see her, but that's all right.

Say goodnight, Mavis.

South of Two Borders,
Down Mexico Way

I think it was about mid-January when I finally snapped. Canada had lost its winter wonderland charm. I was fed up with cold snaps, black ice, living under skies of unrelieved battleship grey.

Mostly I was tired of wearing way too many clothes all the time.

So I hied myself to the local travel agent murmuring in a broken monotone, "Heat! Sunshine! Flowers!" as they prized my Visa card from my frozen fingers.

My travel agent sent me to Mexico. To a tiny town called . . . well, I'm not going to say what it's called because it *is* still a tiny town, unscarred by McDonald's, Tim Hortons or billboards shilling for Lotto 6/49. It is a fishing village, and if you get down to the pier early enough in the morning you can buy your fresh dorado or sailfish or tuna right off the boat.

And yes, there was heat, sunshine and flowers everywhere you looked.

There were other things not customary to the Canuck eye as well. I was about to cool my feet in a small stream one afternoon when a Mexican came toward me wagging his finger.

"*No! No! Aquí cocodrilos!*" he hissed.

Cocodrilos? I thought. Huh. Sounds a lot like the English word . . .

And that's when I looked a little closer at the log I was going to sit down on to take off my socks.

The log was a saltwater crocodile. As long as a Buick.

People there are closer to real life than most Canucks would be comfortable with. A shopkeeper apologized for opening his shop late one day. It was because of *la serpiente* crossing the road, he explained.

A boa constrictor. Also as long as a Buick.

And then there were the *alacranes*. My landlady cautioned me to always check my shoes and shake my clothes before I put them on "*por los alacranes.*" Scorpions. Their sting won't kill you, but you may wish it had.

That said, I must say I never saw a single boa constrictor or scorpion during my stay. But their presence does tilt one toward a . . . heightened awareness. No bad thing for a visitor benumbed by a Canadian winter.

I made the usual *gringo* blunders. Arrived with a suitcase bulging with jackets, sweaters, extra pairs of long pants, woolly socks and shoes.

I spent ninety percent of my time wearing the same baggy shorts accessorized by a pair of Canadian Tire plastic thong slippers.

Two great things about southern Mexico: the people are disarmingly friendly, and the currency is dead simple. When it comes to converting money all you have to do is move the decimal point one place to the left. A hundred pesos? Ten dollars. Twenty-five pesos? Two and a half bucks.

That's two and a half bucks American. To convert to Canadian, you need, as usual, access to Hammurabi's Code.

It was a remarkably indolent vacation I passed down Mexico way, watching the sun go down over the salt-frosted rim of a margarita glass.

Pointless. Non-career-enhancing. Inherently worthless. Utterly without redeeming social value.

I highly recommend it.

II

III

MEANDERING, MELLIFLUOUS WORDS

A Poplolly with Mubblefubbles

*I never write metropolis for seven cents because
I can get the same price for city. I never write
policeman because I can get the same money for
cop.*

—Mark Twain

The author of *The Adventures of Tom Sawyer* and *The Adventures of Huckleberry Finn* was a very funny man, but he was no chucklehead, especially when it came to the business of writing. He knew that words were the currency and coinage of his craft. He also knew that bigger didn't necessarily mean better.

But mostly what Mark Twain did was carry on a lifelong love affair with words.

You pretty well have to, if you want to be a writer. It comes with the territory. Not that you have to be a writer to love words. I know a plumber who does the cryptic crossword in the *New York Times* every day. And I know a farmer who reads Homer in the original Greek. Lots of people love words. In fact a chap by the name of Vick Knight, Jr., has published a book called

My Word, which is devoted to the favourite words of famous people.

Ronald Reagan claimed his favourite word was "home." For Billy Graham it's "decision." Lucille Ball voted the word "beauty" as the most . . . well, beautiful word in the language. For writer Erma Bombeck it was "yes."

Some of the people Knight queried followed the lead of Mark Twain (see above). Which is to say that they reacted with a certain stinginess. Playwright Ira Levin sent a telegram that read "Sorry, I'm in the middle of a play and need every word I've got." Science fiction writer Isaac Asimov wrote a reply in longhand. It read, "I thought about your request and I really don't have a favourite word and even if I make one up, it will mean getting a picture to you, and making up some soppy paragraph or other, and—well, I just don't want to."

It's a tougher question than it appears on the surface. What would you pick as your favourite word? The English language is festooned (there's one of my favourites) with hundreds of potential delegates.

Someone once asked Willard Espy for a list of his favourite words. The famous wordsmith replied with meandering, mellifluous, wisteria, Shenandoah, murmuring . . . and gonorrhea.

Again, words don't have to be lengthy to be splendid. Hush is a wonderful word. So is mist. And dawn.

Many good words have, alas, been lost. Back in the sixteenth century, a pretty young woman was called a bellibone or a poplolly. And someone who was down in the dumps was said to be suffering a bad case of mubblefubbles.

I'd be hard-pressed to say what my favourite word is. Ugly words are plentiful enough. Victual is an ugly word. So is saxophone. And phlegmatic. Ugly is easy, but most beautiful?

Maybe I'll go with Dorothy Parker. Someone once asked the New York wit what she thought was the most beautiful phrase in the English language. Ms. Parker smiled and murmured, "Cheque enclosed."

Emilion Laughs

What's in a name? old Bill Shakespeare once famously wrote. Answer: plenty.

Take the case of a convicted bank robber in Adelaide, Australia who is now free and walking the streets. He was in the slammer serving a ten-year sentence until a criminal court judge ruled that the jury that convicted the man might have been unduly and subconsciously influenced by his given name. The judge overturned the unanimous verdict and ordered the man released forthwith. The crook's name? Rob.

Rob Banks.

Sometimes there's justice. Sometimes people get the names they deserve. The actress Audrey Hepburn was married to a Swiss psychiatrist with the endearing name of Dr. Dotti. There's a gas station attendant in Hatteras, North Carolina, who answers to the name of Wheeler Balance. And there's a famous religious prelate in the Philippines known to all the world as Cardinal Sin. If you have access to a Greater Manhattan telephone book you can look up a chap in the West Sixties who is listed as Mr. Pleasant Finch. And if there's any justice there, he's a birdwatcher.

Sometimes you have to wonder what people were thinking when they named their kids. There's a student in New Zealand who must live with the name Genghis Cohen, and another college freshman at Williams College in Massachusetts whose driver's licence identifies him as Warren Peace.

I know of a resident of the Midwest who would swap names with either of them in a heartbeat. His (or her) name?

Katz Meow.

Animals often bear the brunt of our penchant for handing out goofy names. The Algonquin Hotel wit Dorothy Parker named her pet canary Onan, "because he spills his seed on the ground." There's an aardvark at the London Zoo whose name-plate identifies him as Emilion.

Why Emilion? Don't you remember the old Al Jolson hit?

> *Aardvark Emilion miles*
> *for one of your smiles*
> *my Mammmmmmy!*

Sorry.

There's really no limit when it comes to silly names. There's a practising attorney at law in Los Angeles named Lake Trout.

And he has a brother named Brook.

Of course you don't have to put up with the name your parents gave you. Some people are willing to go to the trouble and expense of legally changing their name. A certain Mr. A. Przvbysz of Detroit, grew tired of the hassles caused by his over-consonanted handle, so he changed it. He now answers to Mr. C. Przvbysz.

Humperdinck Fangboner. Theodolphus J. Poontang. Mrs. Maginis Oyster. Marmalade P. Vestibule—there's no end of weird monikers. My overall favourite? It's hard to choose, but it's also hard to beat a dowager who lives in North Carolina named Melissy Dalciny Caldony Yankee Pankee Devil-Take-The-Irish Garrison.

But even the simplest names can cause serious embarrassment. I've got a friend by the name of Jack Jones. Simple name, right? What kind of trouble could come out of a name like that?

I found out one time when I spotted him striding through the arrivals level at Terminal Two of Toronto Pearson International Airport. Hadn't seen him for years, but he was walking fast in the opposite direction.

So naturally, I yelled at the top of my lungs, "Hi, Jack!"

Caution! Tourists Ahead!

So, did you go to Paris for your vacation?
I dunno. My wife bought the tickets.

Brace yourself, Canada. It is spring at long last; our splendid nation looks more beautiful and peaceful than ever, and the Canadian loonie is still worth just a hair more than a plugged nickel. Such a divine convergence of phenomena can signal but one thing.

The annual tidal run of tourists is just around the corner.

Don't get me wrong, I've got nothing against tourism. It's a decent enough way for a country to turn a buck, certainly better than clear-cutting a province, throwing up another box store mega-mall or draining a Great Lake.

I like tourists. I really do. Their credit cards and wallets are welcome any time at all.

But . . . do they have to be so dumb? Tourists, I mean. Do they put their brains in cold storage before they cross the border? Not all of them, of course. Some visitors are smarter than, say Al Capone. When asked if he smuggled booze from Canada, he replied, "I don't even know what street Canada is on."

On the other hand, some tourists make old Scarface look like Bertrand Russell. A travel agent I know told me of a phone call he took last year.

"I want to complain about Air Canada," the caller told him. Join the queue, the agent thought, but replied, "What's the problem, madam?"

"Weight discrimination," she huffed. "I was flying from Toronto to California and the ticket agent put a tag on my luggage that says FAT. I know I'm a bit overweight, but I won't stand for that kind of ridicule."

"Ah, where were you flying to in California, ma'am?"

"Fresno," replied the caller.

The travel agent put her on hold, laughed until he cried, composed himself, picked up the phone and said, "FAT is the baggage code for Fresno, ma'am. I'm sure Air Canada meant . . . nothing personal."

A tourist information office in Victoria, BC, recorded the following queries:

How much do your totem poles grow every year?

Are there any dogsled rental outlets in Victoria?

I'm calling about this Kill-A-Whale thing. What do you do with them after you've killed them?

And, after being quoted a package tour price in Canadian funds:

How many US dollars in a fund?

I'd like to get smug and sanctimonious about the intelligence differential between savvy Canadians and gormless Americans but there's a story in my family about an uncle (relax, Aunt Eunice, I won't name him) who went with a busload of tourists on a tour of Runnymede in England.

"And this," intones the tour guide, "is the spot where the barons forced King John to sign the Magna Carta."

My uncle pipes up, "When did that happen?"

"1215," answers the guide.

My uncle looks at his watch and says, "Damn! Missed it by half an hour!"

How to Outheckle Hecklers

One of the things I do when I'm not playing hunt and peck with my computer keyboard is speechify. Which is to say I stand up on my hind legs in front of roomfuls of strangers and try to make them laugh.

It's not an unpleasant gig, once you get over stage sweats. Public speakers get to travel all over the country; you meet plenty of folks you otherwise wouldn't, plus you get a nice speaker's fee and usually a free dinner out of the deal.

Of course there is a downside to making public speeches. It is called The Heckler.

It's an uncommon breed, but there only needs to be one of them in an audience of hundreds to ruin a speaker's evening. Contrary to the aura of easy confidence good speakers exude, they're usually sweating bullets up there. Fear of public speaking is the number one phobia, way ahead of fear of heights and fear of snakes. When a speech is going well, the speaker is like a tightrope walker, still scared but getting across. When some buffoon in the third row yells something, it's like having your tightrope wobble. You know you are millimetres away from freefall.

Fortunately hecklers tend to belong to one of two subspecies: stoned or stunned. A drunken heckler usually has just the one arrow in his quiver. Once that's shot, he's roadkill. The stupid ones are more difficult. For one thing, they don't appreciate how stupid they are. Luckily the audience usually does. Audiences, by and large, are incredibly forgiving organisms. They don't like hecklers any more than the speaker does. And if the speaker says something—pretty much anything—that puts the heckler in his place, the audience will rise and cheer as one.

I've never found the perfect squelch for hecklers, but other speakers have handled the situation deftly. Some boob once made the mistake of interrupting David Letterman in mid-monologue. Letterman paused, surveyed the heckler through hooded eyes and murmured, "What exactly is on your mind, if you'll excuse the exaggeration?"

I know a stand-up comedian who skewers males (hecklers are almost always male, and isn't that a surprise?) with "Ah! Good to see you again, back in men's clothing."

If he doesn't feel like toying with the heckler, he dismisses him with "I'm sorry sir, I don't speak alcoholic."

Or, "You'll have to forgive me, I don't know how to deal with you. I'm a comedian, not a proctologist."

And if he's really ticked off, he yells at the heckler, "Save your breath. You'll need it to inflate your date later."

Crude retorts, but we live in crude times. Our ancestors, not surprisingly, handled hecklers with much better grace. The author Charles Lamb was once interrupted during a reading by a heckler who hissed at him. Lamb paused, skewered the interloper with his gaze and purred, "There are only three creatures that hiss: a goose, a snake and a fool. Stand forth so that we may identify you."

Sir Robert Menzies, one-time Prime Minister of Australia, was once beset at a political rally by a woman heckler.

"I wouldn't vote for you if you were the Archangel Gabriel!" she shrieked.

Menzies calmly replied, "If I were the Archangel Gabriel, madam, you would scarcely be in my constituency."

Ah, but my all time favourite heckler put-down sprang from the lips of a British political troublemaker by the name of John Wilkes. Mr. Wilkes stepped on a lot of toes during his eighteenth-century political career, including a pair of bunioned beauties attached to the Earl of Sandwich. Wilkes and the Earl cordially loathed each other and took every opportunity to so testify. One evening after a boozy dinner, the Earl rounded on Wilkes and thundered, "Egad, Wilkes! I have often wondered what catastrophe would bring you to your end. I think that you shall die of the pox [i.e. syphilis] or the noose."

And quick as a cobra, Wilkes stood up, smiled silkily and retorted, "That would depend, My Lord, on whether I embraced your mistress or your principles."

I'd give up my speaker's fee to get off a squelch like that.

The Ballbearing Invasion

Kids say the darndest things.

—Art Linkletter

They certainly do, and nobody knows it better than the star-crossed professionals who get to spend most of their working hours with our kids—their teachers. Teachers get to mark tests and examinations, and that's where the teachers learn that some kids don't retain information quite as efficiently as others. Hence the student blooper phenomenon. Herewith a collection of some of the more outrageous howlers committed to paper by our little darlings.

Science with a vengeance:

"We get our temperature in different ways. Either fairinheit, cellcius, or centipede."

"One horsepower is the amount of energy it takes to drag a horse five hundred feet in one second."

"A molecule is so small it can't be observed by the naked observer."

Famous people of science don't escape the swipe of bloopism. One student wrote that the law of gravity was passed by Isaac

Newton, while another insisted that the Russian Pavlov was famous for studying the salvation of dogs.

Young students seem to have an even shakier grasp of biology. In a class report one child wrote, "Our biology class went out to explore the swamp and to collect little orgasms." And another juvenile chronicler recorded, "In biology today, we digested a frog."

You want to hope that these kids don't choose a medical career:

"The big artery in your neck is called the jocular vein."

"The pelvis protects the gentiles."

"A permanent set of teeth consists of eight canines, two molars, and eight cuspidors."

"The heart beats faster when you are younger, average when you are middle age, hardly at all when you are old, and not at all when you are dead."

The zounds of music:

"Music sung by two people is called a duel."

"A harp is a nude piano."

"My favourite composer is an opus."

"Agnus Dei was a woman composer famous for her church music."

"A very liked piece is the 'Bronze Lullaby.'"

Putting the litter in literature:

"Shakespeare was famous for writing and performing tragedies, comedies and hysterectomies."

"Shakespeare wrote his plays in Islamic pentameter."

"A great Jewish leader in Scotland was Rabbi Burns."

"I like the story *The Last of the Moccasins*."

"In Ibsen's *Ghosts*, Oswald dies of congenial syphilis."

"Jake Barnes in *The Sun Also Rises* was injured in the groin region and was impudent for the rest of his life."

And then of course there's history, ancient and modern. One student noted that Rome was invaded by the ballbearings. Another explained that the Bolshevik Party was led by John

Lennon. And my favourite, a student commenting on fashion in Ancient Egypt:

"Early Egyptian women wore a garment called a calasirus. It was a sheer dress which started beneath the breasts which hung to the floor."

Man, if that didn't make Egyptian guys impudent, nothing would.

Philistines and Flunkies

Mariposa, as every Canadian school kid eventually learns, is a mythical small town on the shores of Lake Wissanotti, peopled by improbable characters and invented by a Canadian economist, wit and world-renowned humourist named Stephen Butler Leacock.

Except it's not. Mariposa is a very real small town peopled by improbable characters that sits on the narrows between Lake Simcoe and Lake Couchiching. Its real name is Orillia, Ontario, and Stephen Leacock didn't invent it. He just loved it, lived next door to it and wrote about it, employing lavish gobbets of hyperbole, caricature and flat out distortion in order to protect the guilty and avoid libel suits.

But the relationship between Leacock and the town of Orillia was never less than, well, Mariposan. Many Orillians hated Leacock, for a variety of reasons. For one thing he was an academic, which is even worse than being a politician in some small towns. And come harvest time, Leacock liked to travel into Orillia and sell the vegetables he'd grown all summer, which caused the local farmers to get their gotchies in a knot.

And besides making mock of some of Orillia's most prominent citizens, Leacock . . . well . . . he drank, you know. And what's even worse, he didn't seem to feel guilty about the fact that he drank.

Which goes some way to explaining the perverse relationship that seems to exist between the memory of Leacock and the town he made world-famous. Nine years after his death, when the words Leacock and humour were virtually synonymous around the English-speaking world, the Orillia Town Council voted six-to-two against sending a copy of *Sunshine Sketches of a Little Town* to London as a coronation gift to the new queen.

"It's nice to hob-nob with royalty," one civic worthy explained, "but some flunky in Buckingham Palace would just put the book away."

A dozen years after his death, Leacock's magnificent home on the shores of Lake Couchiching was an abandoned ruin, the windows broken and furniture smashed by vandals. Only the efforts of a band of dedicated and lonely volunteers saved the place and restored it to its former glory.

And the Philistines are still at the gates. As a matter of fact, they probably sold the gates for firewood. The town of Orillia gave the green light to a developer allowing him to gobble up most of the land Leacock once owned. Said developer hastily chopped down trees, bulldozed shrubs and paved everything that didn't move. So now when you visit the Leacock homestead you must thread your way through a suburban sprawl of unlikely townhouses straight out of Don Mills. Or Disneyworld.

Ah, Orillia. Home of the most famous humourist Canada ever produced. Orillia. Where the sign at the town limits reads, "Welcome to Orillia, Home of Gordon Lightfoot."

Well, you know one thing. If Stephen Leacock were alive he'd be holding his glass on high, in a toast.

And saying, "Yep, that's Mariposa alright."

Canada: Garden of Babble-On

One thing we all know for sure about Canada—it's a bilingual nation, right? Two languages—French and English—spoken here.

It is to rire.

Open your ears, folks. Canada's not a bilingual nation. It's a polyglot, Tower of Babel nation. Take a stroll through Vegreville, Alberta, and what are you likely to hear? Ukrainian. Order a coffee in the Hoito restaurant in Thunder Bay, and what is the waitress speaking? Finnish. Stroll down the main street of Banff, and chances are fifty-fifty the conversation you hear will be in Japanese.

You can get by speaking Italian in Toronto, Farsi in Vancouver, Icelandic in Gimli and Gaelic in Cape Breton.

Then there's slang and dialects. Joual in Quebec, Michif among many Métis on the Prairies.

And that's not even getting to the languages that were here before the big boats with the white sails came.

Did you know there are over fifty aboriginal languages still spoken in Canada? There's Anishinabe, Inuktitut, Kwakwala, Maliseet, Mi'kmaq, Mohawk, Siksika and Slavey to name a handful. The language names might not be familiar, but I guarantee you already know some words in them.

Saskatchewan, Ontario, Manitoba. Nanaimo, Winnipeg, Ottawa. See? You speak like a pro.

Canada is so rich in languages we've all but lost one without even noticing. A hundred years ago it was the lingua franca of all encounters between West Coast natives and European traders and explorers. It is known as the Chinook jargon.

Not a language really, a few hundred words at most. A little French, a little English and a lot of native words all stirred together. We still have a few nuggets of Chinook jargon in English: the word hootch for homemade liquor comes from *hootchanoo* and snoose for chewing tobacco is a corruption of *chinoos*, the native word for tobacco. We can thank Chinook jargon for the word potlatch, meaning a feast, and for the word muckamuck. We speak of high muckamucks when referring to moguls and tycoons like Conrad Black and Donald Trump. In Chinook jargon, *hyas muckamuck* was a person important enough to eat at the main table with the chief.

Someone once remarked on the unusually large number of pet dogs on the West Coast named Chako. Actually, its not a name. It's Chinook jargon for 'come here.'

And people of all races who live on the West Coast still use the term skookum widely. It's a word with a lot of meanings. It can be good, powerful, delicious, tough or just big.

There's a set of powerful rapids in British Columbia called Skookumchuck. That's pure Chinook: skookum means strong and chuck means ocean.

But nobody on the Pacific coast seems to have much use for a trading language anymore. Aside from a few linguistic fossils, Chinook jargon is as dead as Etruscan or Phoenician.

A pity. We lose some words that would be useful in any language, such as *klahanie*, which means outside. It's tricky though. If you are klahanie, you are in the great outdoors. But if you "go klahanie," you're on your way to the biffy.

Then there's tillicum or tilikum. This refers to kin or people. Tillicums can be your friends, your family or your social group. The word was commonly used to refer to your ally or buddy.

My favourite morsel of lost Chinook jargon? Klahowya. It was the standard thing to say when meeting someone or leaving them, like aloha in Hawaiian. It sounds like a corruption of the English expression "How are you?" but linguists believe it derives from a word in the Chinook language, *klahauia*.

Whatever. To my ear it sounds cheery and salubrious and disarmingly friendly. I can visualize an early explorer—a Fraser or a Vancouver—nervously approaching a group of Salish people and waiting for the magic word.

So. Klahowya, tillicum?

Rock and Roll Reporter

When you turn 35, something happens to the music.

—Gene Lees

How true. Breathe there readers over the age of thirty five who don't pine for the good old music of their youth? And who doesn't think that the songs that make up today's hit parade exhibit all the charm and musicality of a tomcat in rut having his way with a set of bagpipes?

I know that the music I rocked to twenty-five years ago was infinitely superior to the squawking and squalling that comes over my radio today.

Oddly enough, I seem to remember my father making the same point about his music.

Not surprising, I guess. The music we like as kids filtered down to us through a swamp of raging hormones. It's only natural that we outgrow the music. Most of us anyway.

There's always Jane Scott.

Jane is a reporter with a newspaper called the *Cleveland Plain Dealer* in Ohio. The rock and roll scene is her assigned beat. Every Friday and Saturday night finds Jane crammed into a writhing, thrashing mob, listening to groups like Twisted Sister, Smashing Pumpkins or The Dead Kennedys. It's a job she's held for three decades.

Jane Scott, rock and roll reporter, is seventy-seven years old.

"I must be the only rock writer who is going to their sixtieth high school reunion this summer," says Jane.

What does she look like? Like a cross between your grandmother and a bag lady. Silver-grey curls tumble helter-skelter around her heavy horn-rimmed glasses. She wears a rumpled raincoat, a man's wristwatch and she carries a shopping bag looped over the arm that's not holding her ever-present notepad.

"My survival kit," she calls the bag. It carries peanut butter sandwiches, a box of Kleenex, safety pins and—the true sign of a rock and roll veteran—a set of ear plugs. She likes a lot of rock groups but even she will admit they're not all good. Still, she has nothing but raves for the Kinks, Bruce Springsteen and ZZ Top.

There aren't many pop stars Jane Scott hasn't met in her thirty years on the beat. She's joked with Jagger, bantered with the Beach Boys, and spent quality time with The Beatles.

There have been other moments. The last time Springsteen performed in Cleveland he yelled out to the audience "Is Janey here? I want to see her." Even Bob Dylan, the hermit of rock and roll, thaws when Jane Scott is around.

"Four years ago I got an invitation to come backstage at the Palace Theatre the night of his show," recalls Jane. "I did manage a lame question about his album. When I extended my hand to shake good-bye, he kissed me on both cheeks. Later I was told that he dedicated 'Like A Rolling Stone' to me."

How big is Jane Scott in the annals of rock and roll? Big enough to rate her own exhibit in the Rock and Roll Hall of Fame in Cleveland. Right up there along with Aretha Franklin, The Supremes, Eric Clapton, Michael Jackson and Simon and Garfunkel. Jane Scott's listened to and written about them all.

Well, not quite all. Jane Scott does have one regret. She never got to meet The King.

But she came close. Back in the sixties Jane tiptoed up the back stairs to the top floor of the old Hotel Statler, peeked around the corridor and . . .

"The jig was up. Scowling down at me was a bodyguard about seven feet tall with a hairdo like Don King. He seemed four feet wide. I never did get an interview with Elvis Presley."

Elvis's loss.

Pardon Me for Not Rising

The grave's a fine and private place
But none, I think, do there embrace.
                                        —Andrew Marvell

Too true, Andrew. Whatever else the death experience might offer, it does not appear to be a barrel of guffaws. Or, for that matter, a love-in full of hugs and kisses.

Death is a serious and solemn business, and more's the pity. I think death could use a horse laugh or two.

Not to mention a little truth in advertising. Consider epitaphs, those little lines of praise engraved on tombstones supposedly to tell the living a little bit about the departed.

Did you ever read an honest epitaph?

Probably not.

Ambrose Bierce defined an epitaph as "an inscription which hopes that virtues acquired by death will have a retroactive effect."

There's a story told about Charles Lamb, the British writer. Apparently, as a child, Charles was walking through a graveyard with his sister, reading the epitaphs on tombstones, all full of "beloved" thises and "virtuous" thats.

Charles turned to his older sister and asked, "Mary, where are all the naughty people buried?"

Good question. Herewith a compendium of epitaphs, real and imagined that—if they didn't make it to granite immortality—should have.

American wit and writer Dorothy Parker:

Excuse my dust.

George S. Kaufman, American playwright:

Over my dead body!

You don't have to be famous to create an immortal epitaph. Consider this offering from a very plain tombstone in a cemetery in Edinburgh, Scotland:

Beneath this stone a lump of clay
Lies Uncle Peter Dan'els
Who early in the month of May
Took off his winter flannels.

In a Ruidoso, New Mexico cemetery you can find a stone that reads:

Here lies
Johnny Yeast.
Pardon me
For not rising.

An attorney in Rockford, Illinois by the name of John Goembel got the epitaph most lawyers would probably settle for out of court:

Goembel
John E.
1867–1946
The Defence Rests.

And has anyone—poet or magistrate—summed up the hazards of dangerous driving more succinctly than a chiselled tombstone in Uniontown, Pennsylvania?

Here lies the body
of Jonathan Blake
Stepped on the gas
Instead of the brake.

An old maid's gravestone in Scranton Pennsylvania is brutally honest:

No hits, no runs, no heirs.

But for all time, no-nonsense brevity I would have to wave the checkered flag in favour of Arthur Haine of Vancouver, Washington. Mr. Haine was an atheist, it seems, and an unapologetic one at that. His tombstone inscription reads:

Haine
Hain't.

Whatever Happened to the Paperboy?

Okay, so I'm a geezer. But there are certain privileges that come with Geezerhood. I have, for instance, seen things that today's kiddies can scarcely imagine. Things like:

Twelve-inch black and white television sets.

Ice cream cones for six cents.

Horse-drawn milk wagons clanking slowly down the streets.

And kids with paper routes.

Remember them? The kids who delivered the afternoon newspaper to your porch six days a week? The routes themselves are still around, but they're serviced by adults. The kids, for the most part, are long gone—as are the afternoon newspapers, for that matter. Dailies mostly come out in the early morning now. Pretty hard for a kid these days to juggle school classes *and* a paper route.

Pity. A paper route was a great way for kids to get introduced into the workaday world. You found out right quick about things like . . .

Reliability: "It's seven o'clock! You're two hours late with my paper!"

High finance: "Yes, ma'am, you owe $3.16 for the first two weeks of the month, plus $1.10 for last week because there was no paper on Friday, which comes to . . . "

Human frailty: "I'm sorry, sonny, I only have a twenty-dollar bill. Could you come back, ummm, say . . . Thursday?"

You learned all that, plus how to balance 112 copies of the *Star Weekend Edition* in the flimsy carrier on your CCM one-speed without doing a one-and-a-half gainer into the asphalt.

Having a paper route meant unkidlike responsibility. You couldn't always go off with the guys for a spontaneous game of pick-up hockey, because your papers were waiting. You couldn't take that Friday night trip to the cottage until you found a trustworthy pal to deliver your Saturday papers. You often had to deal with snarly dogs or surly customers. (I preferred the dogs.)

But there was a definite plus side. For one thing, you had yourself some actual pocket money. And, if your timing on the route was right, your manners passable and your eyes suitably beseeching, you just might score an ice-cold glass of lemonade from a charitable granny. Even—glory!—a wedge of piping hot apple pie, fresh from the oven.

Now I'm really dating myself. Today that pie would be "fresh" from the microwave, by way of Safeway, the lemonade would be Evian water, and anyway, there'd be nobody to serve it because Granny's in the old folks' home and Mom and Pop are both out working to pay off the mortgage-heat-'n-hydro plus the maxed-out credit cards, not to mention the GST and the PST on everything from nachos to newspapers.

As for our kids these days, well, I hope they've figured out other ways to develop the innate guile you needed to be a prosperous paperboy.

I was okay at it, but my pal Johnny Charlton was the master. I still remember him standing at the corner of Lawrence Avenue and Roxaline Street, hawking his surplus newspapers to passers-by, yelling, "Extra! Extra! Read all about it! Seventeen people swindled!"

And a neighbour—Mr. Rutherford—buys a paper, checks the front page and says, "Hey! There's nothing here about seventeen people being swindled!"

But Johnny doesn't respond. He's too busy yelling "Extra! Extra! Read all about it! Eighteen people swindled!"

From Verse to Worse

Americans are good at inventing heroes that
weren't, like Paul Bunyan and Abner Doubleday.
[Canadians] cancel heroes that really were.
                                              —Axel Harvey

I'm not sure that I entirely agree with Mr. Harvey. Seems to me Canada has an inordinate share of heroes, from Billy Bishop to Mary Pickford, from Roberta Bondar to Terry Fox. We have our literary heroes (Margarets Atwood and Laurence); our musical heroes (Joni Mitchell, Neil Young). We have painter heroes and sculptor heroes; dance heroes and sports heroes.

I'd like to add a new name to the pantheon of Canadian superstardom. Ladies and gentlemen may I nominate Mr. James McIntyre, Canada's—nay, the world's—foremost Poet of Cheese.

McIntyre, like Shakespeare and Dickens, sprang from humble stock. He emigrated to Canada from Scotland in 1841 and settled in southern Ontario. He became a furniture dealer in St. Catherines. But the spark of creativity simmering within the McIntyre breast would not long be denied. Soon McIntyre was limning odes to the world around him: the rustic, dairy-farming countryside of Oxford County, Ontario.

What sort of odes? Herewith a representative stanza from his epic "When to Sell Grain and Produce":

> *Remember too that of your wheat*
> *The rats of it will fondly eat*
> *Sell it and money then invest*
> *And you can get good interest.*

Or consider his lyrical salute to wildlife in "Wild Goose Shot at Midnight Nov., 1888":

> *But when they flew o'er the river Thames*
> *They swooped down to take a dive,*
> *But sport with shot gun at them aims*
> *And one at least did not survive.*

By now you will have surmised that Mr. McIntyre was a bad poet.

No. Mr. McIntyre was a *bad* poet. A spectacularly, five-star, *ne plus ultra*, wretched writer of doggerel that was an affront to the trees cut down to make the paper he wrote it on.

And yet he was published. The editor of the *Toronto Globe* frequently ran McIntyre poems (for comic relief, it's suspected). Even a scribe at the *New York Tribune* confessed to being "amused."

More incredibly, the people of Oxford County adored McIntyre and his musings. He was constantly asked to "deliver a few lines" on all manner of public occasions.

And McIntyre, was only too happy to oblige, be it a wedding, a funeral, a store opening or . . . just cheese.

> *To us it is a glorious theme*
> *To sing of milk, of curds, and cream*
> *Were it collected it could float*

Upon its bosom small steam boat
Cows, numerous as a swarm of bees
Are milked in Oxford to make cheese.
                    —from "Oxford Cheese Ode"

McIntyre, though locally loved, never achieved the international renown he knew he deserved, despite poems written about his "colleagues."

We have scarcely time to tell thee
Of the strange and gifted Shelley
Kind-hearted man, but ill-fated,
So youthful, drowned and cremated.

When McIntyre went to his reward in 1906, he was remembered in verse by his daughter Kate, who wrote:

His book he'd give you gratis
Filled with divine afflatus
And local news;
High on the wall of fame
He hath written out his name,
Inscribed his muse.

Alas, daughter Kate faltered in the footprints of Canada's worst poet, and published no more verse.

Pity. She coulda been a contender.

What's in a Nickname?

Now it can be revealed—my teenaged nickname, I mean. For the last four decades I have answered to Art, Arthur, AB, Mr. Black, Dr. Black and Hey You.

But before that I spent most of my teenaged years cringing under the nickname of Schwartz.

Why Schwartz? Well, one of my boyhood chums discovered that not only was Schwartz the name of a manufacturer of truck mud flaps, it was also German and Yiddish for black. The die was cast. Schwartz I was and Schwartz I would remain until my family mercifully moved to a distant town.

It could have been worse. One of the more hapless kids in our circle was known as Cootie. Another answered, not terribly keenly, to Mouse.

And Doug Howarth became Hogarth, Bobby Hamner became Hammerhead and Harvey Becker became . . .

Don't ask.

Nicknames can be exceedingly cruel, but my, they're popular—at least among the sadists who bestow them on the rest of us. US President Bush (nickname Dubya) is big on nicknames, saddling his underlings with monikers like Pancho, Stretch and Sweet Cheeks.

Because Bush is so, well, bush-league, a lot of his nicknames carry the familiar, ugly sting of the no-class bully. Montezuma is his nickname for Mexican president Vicente Fox, and he referred to staff member Ari Fleischer as his 'bald Jew.' We don't want to even guess what he called Da Liddle Guy From Shawinigan.

Canadian politicians are no strangers to nicknames. We've had Dief the Chief, Old Velcro Lips and Joe Who. Some politicians of course, don't last long enough to earn a nickname.

Stockwell, we hardly knew ye.

Hockey players are popular targets for nicknames—The Great One, the Flower, the Big M, the Rocket. Musicians get tagged too—Satchmo, Fats, Duke, Dizzy, BB and the incomparable Blind Lemon Jefferson.

Not to mention more contemporary contributions like Snoop Doggy Dogg, Puff Daddy and Eminem.

Mobsters get the best nicknames of all. It's hard to improve on Scarface Al, Tony Ducks, Sammy the Bull and Big Tuna.

But I would say the fertile crescent of creative nicknamery would have to be Canada's own Cape Breton Island. It's not a big place, and the name pool is even smaller, consisting of flocks of Mcs and Macs, as befits a piece of the country populated almost exclusively by folks of the Celtic persuasion.

It shouldn't be surprising, then, that down through the years a lot of Cape Bretoners have ended up with the same surnames. What is surprising is the enterprise they show in dealing with any possible confusion.

Donald Cameron is a well-known Canadian writer, but back home in Cape Breton, he's just one of dozens of Donald Camerons. So how to tell him apart? Simple. Donald Cameron the writer is blessed with a shock of prematurely white hair. Hence he becomes Silver Donald Cameron.

Silver Donald gets off lightly. One of his fellow islanders—a miner—has one arm a little longer that the other. His nickname? Alex the Clock. Big hand, little hand—geddit?

Then there's the Cape Breton family descended from an ancestor who loved to spend his spare time gossiping down at the corner store, where his habitual seat of choice was the top of a pickle barrel.

Which is why each and every member of the family is known across the length and breadth of the island—and most likely for all eternity—as one of the Pickle Arse MacLeans.

A fellow by the name of William Hazlitt once wrote that a nickname "is the hardest stone that the devil can throw at a man."

And Hazlitt had never even been to Cape Breton.

Don't Eat Your Tickets

Well, I ain't superstitious, but
a black cat crossed my trail.

— Old blues lyric

I've only been cuffed in the head a few times in my life, and most times I was in a situation where I kind of expected it— doing my level best to cuff somebody else in the head—but I do recall an occasion when a backhander took me by surprise.

I was swabbing decks on an oil tanker somewhere between Halifax and Amuay Bay, Venezuela. I made the mistake of whistling while I swabbed. Next thing I knew, I was sprawled face down on the deck between my bucket and my mop. The bosun, a red-faced Yorkshireman built like a beer stein, stood over me with his hands on his hips.

"Eejit!" he snarled. "Do ye not know better than t'whistle on a ship?"

As a matter of fact I didn't, but I learned right quick. I discovered that among sailors it was considered perilously bad luck to pucker your lips and blow while you're at sea. They believed quite seriously that whistling encouraged the winds to blow.

That wasn't the only superstition those men at sea embraced. They believed it was bad luck to change the name of your boat, to name a boat before it was launched, for two relatives to crew on the same vessel and to board a small boat from any direction but the starboard side.

One crewman told me that sailors never molest seagulls, believing them to be the souls of drowned mariners.

They're a superstitious lot, your sailors, but then why not? They've got a risky job, flitting like water spiders over the tossing bosom of a capricious and frequently violent ocean. They need all the good luck they can get.

Strange how most of us, sailor and landlubber alike, still observe many old superstitions. How many of us would deliberately walk under a ladder? Open an umbrella in the house? Not me. Not without tossing a little salt over my shoulder.

Look at weddings. The bride must wear white. On the wedding day, the groom must not see the bride before she comes down the aisle. And when the deed is done we throw handfuls of confetti or rice at them.

Enduring habits, superstitions. I'm not gullible enough to think that handling toads will give me warts, but I cross my fingers before I go in to ask the boss for a raise.

Mind you, when it comes to superstitions, the Russians make you, me and the entire Canadian merchant marine look like a pack of scientific rationalists. Russians are superstitious with a vengeance.

Give birth to a baby in Moscow and your neighbours will tell you not to show it to strangers for forty days. Bad luck. They also believe it's bad luck to cut the kid's hair or fingernails for a whole year after birth.

In Russia, it is also bad luck to be born or married in May, shake hands over a threshold, give knives or handkerchiefs as gifts or give anybody a half dozen roses.

Five roses are okay. So are seven. Odd numbers are life-affirming. Even numbers mean death.

Russians aren't all negative; they have good luck omens too.

They believe, for example, that if you forget something in the house and have to return for it, you can cancel any accruing bad luck by looking into a mirror and smiling. Before setting out on a trip, superstitious Russians sit down for a minute of silence with friends or family.

And my favourite. On Russian buses you'll often see commuters examining their tickets closely. That's because it's considered the greatest luck if your ticket number happens to have the same three numbers at the beginning and at the end. The thing to do if you get one of those tickets is . . . eat it.

That's right. Eat the ticket. On the spot.

Man. It'll be a long time before I'm desperate enough to eat my bus ticket for luck.

Touch wood.

When a Brand Name Gets Branded

A few years back, a graphic design student woke up with an idea for a brand logo. "Kind of a fat, floating, checkmark," she described it. She sketched it on a notepad and eventually sold it to a sports entrepreneur for fifty bucks.

It was the Nike "swoosh," possibly the most famous brand logo in big business. And Nike is nothing if not big—currently worth nearly five billion dollars US—so big that it could afford to pay ex-basketball star Michael Jordan twenty million dollars a year for endorsements.

Unfortunately Nike largesse is not a worldwide phenomenon. While Jordan hauled down twenty mil annually, the twenty-five thousand Indonesian factory hands who put in eleven-hour days assembling Nike shoes make $2.23 US each.

Per day.

Put at its crudest, Michael Jordan makes more in a year from Nike than twenty-five thousand factory workers combined.

And the markup Nike hauls in on its product is of street-drug proportions. One year a kid in Chicago was murdered for the $225 Nike Air Jordans he had on his feet.

When the shoes left Indonesia they were worth less than ten bucks.

Not surprisingly, Nike has become a little sensitive about the company's image—which helps to explain the exchange of correspondence between Nike and one Jonah Peretti. Mr. Peretti was trying to get in on a Nike promotion that lets customers choose a word or phrase which Nike then stitches on their shoes right under the trademark swoosh.

All right, thought Mr. Peretti. He sent in his order asking that the word "sweatshop" be stitched on his shoes. He got this reply:

> *Your Nike ID order was cancelled for one or more of the following reasons:*
> *(1) It contains another party's trademark or other intellectual property.*
> *(2) It contains the name of an athlete or team we do not have the legal right to use.*
> *(3) It was left blank.*
> *(4) It contains profanity or inappropriate slang.*
> *Thank you, Nike ID.*

Mr. Peretti wrote back pointing out that "sweatshop" was not another party's trademark, the name of an athlete, a blank or a profanity. "I chose this ID because I wanted to remember the toil and labour of the children who made my shoes. Could you please ship them to me immediately."

Nike wrote back insisting that "sweatshop" was inappropriate slang.

Peretti responded that it was a legitimate word found in Webster's Dictionary since 1892. "Your website advertises that the Nike ID program is 'about freedom to choose and freedom to express who you are' . . . I hope you will value my freedom of expression and reconsider your decision to reject my order."

Nike once again turned him down, this time for unspecified reasons and added: "If you wish to reorder your Nike ID product with a new personalization please visit us again at www.nike.com."

And Jonah Peretti replied, "Thank you for the time and energy you have spent on my request. I have decided to order the shoes with a different ID, but I would like to make one small request.

"Could you send me a colour snapshot of the ten-year-old Vietnamese girl who made my shoes?"

No response from Nike as we went to press.

What Else We Lost

In the science-fiction novel *Sirens of Titan*, Kurt Vonnegut suggested that the whole point of human civilization on Earth—from crouching in caves to cruising through deep space—had been to facilitate the delivery of a spare part for a stranded spaceship from another planet.

It's a bit of a stretch, but I feel that way about TV now. And by "now" I mean ever since the morning of Tuesday, September 11, 2001 AD.

I don't normally watch daytime TV if I can avoid it, but the radio program I usually listen to wasn't delivering the customary news, weather and sports that morning. Instead the host was repeating something heretical in radio circles. He was telling listeners to turn on the TV. So I did.

I remember flicking "power" on the remote and seeing two shiny office towers loom up on the screen, one of which seemed to be billowing smoke. The next thing I was conscious of was swallowing and finding it curiously painful. That's because my mouth was dry. It had been hanging open for close to an hour.

I wasn't glued to what you'd call sophisticated TV, just a static shot, no clever pans or zoomy close-ups. And the commentators . . . well, if they were commentating, you scarcely heard them. On the station I was watching, they didn't even comment when the North Tower of the World Trade Centre feathered down off the screen.

Either they assumed they were having technical difficulties with the New York television feed, or they simply couldn't process what their eyes were telling them. When the South Tower came down fifteen minutes later, they acknowledged it, but quietly, almost reverently. I think they realized that no words were necessary. That in fact words weren't up to the job.

But simple TV was up to the job. It was a stupendous, horrifying, crazy-making time to be watching a television set. That's what makes me think that perhaps TV at that moment reached an equivalent point in history as human civilization's rendezvous with the spaceship accessory in Vonnegut's novel. That perhaps we had to endure all those endless seasons of *Wheel of Fortune* and Jerry Springer, *Days of Our Lives* and Jimmy Swaggart, Milton Berle and *Survivor*—maybe we had to go through all that so that TV could be up and running when it really mattered. When for one instant, the entire sighted world was hard-wired into one colossal optic nerve. Fused together by an image of two towers shining against a painfully blue sky.

And then . . . not.

Virtually everyone on earth with access to a TV has seen those images by now. You. Me. Aunt Millie. The Dalai Lama. Osama bin Laden.

Bin Laden, though not claiming authorship of the deed, nevertheless is reported to have fallen to his knees and thanked Allah when informed of it.

Which is why I have moved from having a dim and distant feeling of repugnance for Mr. bin Laden to fervently wishing to see him and all who slither with him reduced to a black, smoking crater in the earth's crust.

And that was the ultimate obscene legacy of September 11's unspeakable horror. The second strike, if you will.

I had—Buddha, God and Allah help me—begun to think like Osama bin Laden.

III

III

NATURE BATS LAST

Canada's Secret Weapon

Could we be serious about the beaver for a moment?

The business of choosing a national mascot is important, and most countries treat it with appropriate solemnity. After all, a national mascot tells the rest of the world which characteristics a nation holds dear. Hence most countries choose mascots that are brave, intelligent, powerful or in some other way dominant and admirable. The US opted for a ferocious bald eagle, wings aflare and talons flashing. Britain reveres a doughty bulldog with a spiked collar and a gobful of wicked-looking teeth. France lines up behind an Amazonian, barricade-bestriding goddess named Marianne. Russia has the burly bear, Costa Rica the magnificent jaguar.

And Canada? Canada has a rat.

Castor canadensis, to be precise. A bottom-feeding pond dweller with buck teeth, a furry spare tire and a tail that looks like it was run over by a Winnebago.

Our national mascot is not noticeably heroic, muscular, clever or oversupplied with sex appeal. That might lead you to think that Canada placed last in the national mascot sweepstakes.

Don't kid yourself. Bucky Beaver may look like a loser, but he is taking over the world as I write.

Don't believe me? Ask the Russians. Away back in the fifties somebody in Finland—a serious vodka enthusiast, I suspect—

got the bright idea of bringing in a brace of Canadian beavers and turning them loose in the Finnish wilderness.

The Canuck imports settled right in, booting out the local European beaver population (they were really kind of wussy) and started to do the two things Canadian beavers do best: making dams and making little beavers.

They made a lot of little beavers. Before long, offspring from those first Canadian migrants were paddling inexorably toward Sweden to the west and Russia to the east. Today Russian biologists glumly reckon there are at least twenty thousand Canadian beavers building unrequested water management projects in northwest Russia. And they're expanding ever southward.

Think about it: the Canadian beaver stands poised to take Moscow, something even Napoleon couldn't do.

You'd think Finlanders might have learned from the Argentinian experience. Back in the forties Argentina imported twenty-five breeding pairs in an attempt to create a fur industry down there. The beavers liked the Argentine outback even more than the European backwoods, and responded in their characteristic beaverian way. Right now, Argentina is smothered in upwards of fifty thousand industrious ex-Canadian dam-builders.

And Britain? Don't even mention Canadian beavers in Britain. Recently some environmentalists in London suggested purchasing some Canadian beavers to reintroduce the animal into the English countryside, where they've been extinct for at least a millennium.

The British press went nuts. "Keep the furry thugs in Canada," one editorial huffed. Another called them "loutish interlopers" and "uncivilized brutes."

Scary. They don't even talk about our hockey players that way.

So is there nothing that can stop a full-scale beaver invasion? Well, there is one antidote, but it's even scarier. This Anti-Beaver Initiative was created here in Canada, fittingly enough. On a prairie farm belonging to eighty-seven-year-old Tom Harper.

Tom had a beaver problem. They plugged his creek and

flooded his fields. Looked like they might even flood him out of house and home if something wasn't done.

Tom tried everything. He called the authorities; they yawned. He set the dogs loose; the beavers swam away. He set live traps; the beavers ignored them. He even tried shooting them. Big deal. There were plenty more where they came from.

In desperation Tom Harper set up loudspeakers near the principal beaver dam. He hooked the speakers up to his radio and . . . he tuned the radio dial to CBC Radio One and cranked up the volume.

CBC Radio One. News and interviews followed by more news and more interviews. Documentaries on gay, lesbian, aboriginal, transsexual, dyslexic, post modern or postpartum issues. Round-table discussions on: The Kyoto Accord. Whither the NDP? Senate Reform. And—no connection—Greenhouse Gas.

CBC Radio One. Twenty-four-seven. The beavers lasted two weeks before they waddled into the prairie wilderness, never to be seen or heard from again.

So, yes, the beaver can be bested. But there is such a thing as cruel and unusual punishment.

Long Live the Windypuff!

One man's weed is another man's flower.

—Anonymous

A recent headline in the *Globe and Mail* shows just how disconnected we've become from the planet we live on. "Springtime Battle with Yellow Menace May be Over," it reads.

It's talking about dandelions.

Dandelions? Yellow menace? The story under the headline crows about a team of Canadian scientists who have discovered a naturally occurring but hitherto unnoticed fungus. The scientists believe this discovery could be a knockout punch for the dandelion. It's a mould that attaches itself to the dandelion plant and feeds off it until the dandelion dies. Once the dandelion is gone, the mould dies too. Sounds ideal, until you ask the question: how come we're killing dandelions in the first place?

Do we kill them because they're ugly? Hardly. The dandelion is a beautiful plant, be it young and golden or old and silvery. Because we think they're noxious? If so, we're pretty stupid. Native people have known for eons that the dandelion is powerful medicine. Even the Puritans purposely packed dandelion seeds when they came to North America so that they could take advantage of its medicinal benefits in the New World.

And the beneficial properties are considerable. In fact it may just be the most nutritionally potent plant growing inside or outside our gardens. Dandelions are full of iron. They provide more potassium than bananas, more beta carotene than carrots and more lecithin than soybeans.

Other countries recognize dandelions' value and deliberately cultivate them as a kitchen staple. And why not? The leaves of young dandelion plants are delicious, and about ten times more nutritious than lettuce. Dandelions make excellent wine, and you can even grind up the tap root to make a coffee substitute. So why do we hate this plant so?

Partly because of our lawn fetish. Somewhere along the way we developed the completely irrational notion that we ought to surround our houses and public buildings with a monotonous carpet of undifferentiated green. Something that grew really fast so we could spend lots of leisure time humping roaring, fume-spewing lawnmowers over it, trying to keep it short.

The dandelion scoffs. We spend small fortunes on lawn rollers, fertilizers, aerators and mutant grass seed, only to wake up one morning to an invasion of gaily waving yellow heads that seem to say, "We're baaaack!"

Then there are the herbicides. North American lawn freaks spend millions of bucks each year mainlining chemical poisons designed to eradicate the dandelion and its kin. Nobody's quite sure what else we're killing, but hey—as long as we get rid of those damn dandelions, eh?

Maybe that's the good news about this new antidandelion fungus: at least it'll get us off our herbicide addiction. My guess is it'll be about as effective as all the other things we've tried in our war on the dandelion. Which is to say, not very.

Call it a butterchin, a windypuff, a fairy clock, a blowball, a dumble-dor or an Irish daisy. Call it what you will, the dandelion is here to stay.

You can't keep a good weed down.

A Parrot is a Man's Best Fiend

You're familiar with the classic Monty Python parrot skit, right? Where John Cleese comes into a pet shop with a dead parrot and tries to get his money back?

It's a very funny skit except for one thing—the premise. What sane, rationally operating human would ever complain about having a parrot that died?

A dead parrot is the only kind of parrot I'd ever consider owning.

I know some people love the birds, but they suffer from a disadvantage: they never met Sydney. Sydney was the name of the parrot I once, it is to laugh, owned. At least that's what I thought the shop owner called him. I believe now that it was a mispronunciation of "Satan." Sydney/Satan was a scarlet macaw: beak by Jimmy Durante, wardrobe by Pimps "R" Us. He was gaudy— all flaming red plumage with blue-green accessory feathers and beady black-pupilled stoplight-yellow eyes that never seemed to blink. Sydney was—I have to admit it—beautiful in his own Boy George way. He was also The Pet From Hell.

"Does your parrot talk?" curious guests would inquire as they peered at Sydney, slouching like Brando in *The Wild Ones*, resplendent and insouciant on his perch.

Talk? No. Sydney did not "talk." Sydney screamed. Louder than a jackhammer. More piercingly than a Skilsaw striking a spike. More excruciatingly than a bevy of F-18s in mid-flypast. Sydney was *loud.*

He was also a tyrant. He transformed my feisty border collie into a shuffling Yowsah mutt the very afternoon they met. I never did learn what he did to my cat, but the poor beast went outside to live in the hedge shortly after Sydney arrived. She still wouldn't come in six weeks after Sydney departed.

Sydney's beak was more powerful than a set of bull clippers. He ate the spines off seven volumes of my *Encyclopaedia Britannica* and severed the phone chord in three places. He chewed up the door trim and uprooted a jade plant onto the living room carpet just, I believe, to watch it die. In his brief gangbang of my life that parrot managed to trash my home, traumatize my family and estrange us from the next-door neighbours.

My dictionary defines "parricide" as the killing of a close relative, but for me, parricide is an act I would have performed, with relish and bare hands, on a certain bird had not Fate, in the form of Sydney's former owner, taken the beast away.

Oh, well. Could have been worse, I suppose. Could have been Flounder. Flounder is a Rainbow Lorie currently living in the Humane Society Animal Shelter in Charlotte, North Carolina. He's tiny, gorgeous . . . and he's got a mouth on him like Blackbeard the Pirate. This is a truly foul fowl. He uses the S-word. He uses several B-words. He uses the F-word so often it's boring.

Flounder has also picked up some charming routines somewhere along his checkered flight path. He lures newcomers to his cage and then shrieks, "Get away from me, you %*&^#+*@%-!" He's turned simple defecation into a form of military assault. He can nail you with Gatling gun guano from a metre away.

His most embarrassing party trick? Waiting until anyone in the shop sits down, whereupon Flounder makes a sound like passing gas and follows it with "Excuuuuuuuuuse me."

Reminds me of a story about another foul-mouthed parrot purchased by an unwitting Saskatoon dowager. It wasn't until she got it home that the lady realized the bird was . . . tainted.

It sang ribald songs. It told dirty jokes. It screamed swear words that Eddie Murphy doesn't know.

Which was a problem, what with the vicar coming to tea that very afternoon. The lady tossed a bed sheet over the birdcage; the bird sang four unexpurgated verses of "Mademoiselle from Armentières." The lady screamed at the parrot to hush; the parrot told the lady to perform an unnatural act. In desperation, for she could hear the vicar's footsteps at the door, the woman snatched the parrot and threw him in the freezer.

A half-hour later, after the vicar's departure, the woman opened the freezer and found the parrot standing there, shivering slightly but decidedly amenable.

"Are you all right?" she asked.

"Fine, ma'am, thank you for asking," said the parrot humbly.

"But you seem so quiet," said the dowager. "Is there anything wrong?"

"Nothing at all, ma'am," said the parrot. "I couldn't be happier.

"But I was just wondering—could you tell me . . . what it was the turkey did?"

Balm in Gilead

"Is there—is there Balm in Gilead?—tell me—
tell me I implore!"
Quoth the raven, "Nevermore."

I was haunted for years by those lines from Edgar Allan Poe's poem, "The Raven." Haunted because (a) I couldn't find Gilead on any CAA road map, and (b) I didn't know what balm Poe was talking about. Lip balm I knew. That's the goop you smeared on your kisser if it was chapped. The atom, hydrogen and plutonium varieties I knew, but I was pretty sure a smart cookie like Mr. Poe would know the difference between b-a-l-m and b-o-m-b.

My confusion was compounded when I moved to Northwestern Ontario and found myself covered with sticky green buds one otherwise lovely spring afternoon. My neighbour, a veteran bushworker, laughed and slapped his brawny thigh in delight.

"Bin standin' under a bamagilleum tree, haintcha?"

Bamagilleum tree? What the hell was a bamagilleum tree? I asked a forester friend.

"It's the balm of Gilead tree he's talking about. The locals call them bamagilleums."

Fine. But I still didn't know what Gilead or balm meant.

Until I checked the Bible and found out that Edgar Allan was actually quoting the old prophet Jeremiah who asked the same question (though not of a raven) in Jer. 8:22.

Balm is a simple contraction of balsam. Which comes full circle when you realize the bamagilleum tree that had me buffaloed is actually a variety of balsam poplar. Balsam from Gilead was a kind of Biblical cure-all, supposed to be good for whatever ailed you.

Which brings me, finally, to the point of all this scribbling. If you happen to run into Edgar Allan Poe down at the tavern this afternoon, would you pass on this message:

There is balm in Gilead.

Archeologists excavating the rocky slopes overlooking the Dead Sea oasis of Ein Gedi in Israel have uncovered the ruins of a massive watchtower, its entrance jammed shut with a giant round stone. Behind that stone lies the secret of Ein Gedi: a prized balsam oil, so rare it was used to anoint Hebrew kings as early as the seventh century BC. The leader of the archeology team, Yizhar Hirschfeld, is sure the secret is in there. "Nothing like this has been found anywhere in the ancient world," he says.

Apparently the smell was beyond sublime. The Roman historian Pliny the Elder called it the finest in the world, as did many Jewish chroniclers.

So exactly how seductive was the balm of Gilead?

We don't know. The trees from which the oils were extracted became extinct about fifteen hundred years ago. So we don't have any balm of Gilead to smell, but that doesn't mean we won't have some soon.

The archeologists hope to analyze samples scraped from the ancient Ein Gedi vats from which the famous balm of Gilead can be reconstituted and no doubt, put on the market to fight it out with Brut, Mennen and Arid Extra Dry.

But they might want to think twice about it. The Jews of Ein Gedi were famous for only one thing, the fragrant balm they produced. And they guarded their secret with fanatical care. In fact the archeologists also uncovered a centuries-old inscription on the floor of a synagogue in the ancient town. It reads, "Cursed be he who reveals the secret of the village."

I'm not superstitious, but if I was in Yizhar Hirschfeld's desert boots, I'd think hard before I got involved in remarketing balm of Gilead as a roll-on deodorant.

And Yizhar, if some night you answer a rap on the door and find a raven standing there, I'd forget the project altogether.

Is That a Pig Spleen in Your Pocket?

I want to reassure everyone that this is *not* going to turn into a rant about Environment Canada weather forecasts.

I am *not* going to dwell on the fact that despite umpty gazillion dollars worth of thermometers, barometers, anemometers, radar, Doppler, weather balloons and interstellar meteorological satellites Environment Canada is almost always *dead wrong* about predicting temperatures and conditions in the microclimate that surrounds my house.

I will *not* point out that the Environment Canada spokesperson *never admits* his or her organization screwed up the day after it rains when it was supposed to have been sunny, or when a force-ten gale shows up on what was forecast as a calm day.

I am just going to say that when it comes to weather forecasting Gus Wickstrom of Tompkins, Saskatchewan, does it better. What's more, Gus doesn't have a high-tech laboratory full of sophisticated instruments and gauges.

He does his forecasting with pig spleens.

You read right. Gus takes the spleen from a slaughtered pig (older hogs are best), holds it out in front of him, palpates the organ, sometimes even takes a little chomp of it ("I like to bite into it a little . . . I am trying to be more accurate") . . .

And then Gus Wickstrom predicts the weather for Tompkins, Saskatchewan, and environs.

Is he any good at it? The *Farmer's Almanac* thinks so. The magazine, which is mildly famous for the accuracy of its own weather forecasts, extolled Gus Wickstrom and his pig spleens in a feature article not long ago. He gets calls from radio stations and TV stations around the continent, asking him to tell the world what the weather's going to be.

He's been interviewed by media outlets in New York and Los Angeles. KOMO TV recently flew him in to Seattle to read his pig spleen prognostications for Washington.

It's amazing what Gus can suss out from a simple pig spleen. "The last few years there's been a blue streak at the bottom of the spleens," says Gus. "That tells me we'll get some rain in May and June. [This year's] spleens have a good layer of fat compared to last year and that usually indicates more moisture."

Is Gus on the money or is he just talking through his pork-bellies? Well, last year he went toe to toe with the official Canadian weather office—and mopped the floor with them.

"Environment Canada has thousands and thousands of dollars worth of equipment," says Gus, "and last year they said it would be cold and wet [in the Prairies].

"But the spleens showed exactly the opposite, and that's what we got—a warm and mild winter with little precipitation."

Environment Canada has a bit of an excuse in this contest—they've only been around for a few decades. Spleen-reading goes back for generations.

"It came from my dad's side of the family," says Gus. "They came to Saskatchewan from Sweden back in the early nineteen-hundreds. But weather predictions with spleens were done in Stockholm long before that."

Gus has great respect for a body organ that doesn't get a lot of positive press, generally speaking. He says the spleen is a powerful piece of meat that can do much more than tell you if it's going to rain on your parade. He says slapping a chunk of raw spleen on your balding head promotes hair growth.

"I often wear it under my hat when I go to check the mail," he says. He's a big fan of taking spleen internally too. Gus reckons a feed of spleen is good for folks with rheumatism, arthritis, bad hearing, failing eyesight.

"It can put a little zip in your life," he says. Speaking of which, Gus cautions against eating too much spleen. He says a little under 120 grams a day is the absolute maximum. Why? Because spleen is . . . well, as Gus said, powerful.

"It acts like Viagra. Anyone can eat it—men or women—but there is no use only one spouse eating it since that person will overpower the other."

Aha.

That explains that famous old Prairie expression: "Is that a pig spleen in your pocket or are you happy to see me?"

Fire Away!

Once the forest fire season finally winds down, the fall rains snuff out whatever's still smoldering. Before long most of Canada's vast boreal forests are snuggled under a flameproof blanket of white stuff.

Forest firefighters finally get to take off their boots and relax for a spell, and no doubt spend some time shaking their heads over the fire season they've just been through. There's a new enemy out there nowadays, particularly for the pilots of water bombers.

Boaters.

And I'm not talking about a couple of old duffers out fly-casting from a dory in the middle of a lake. I'm talking about the newest water sport: boaters who drag race with the water bombers.

It sounds insane, but it's true. Water bomber pilots are reporting increasing numbers of boaters who come, like cluster flies, every time a bomber descends to scoop water from a lake.

It's a game that's unbelievably stupid and potentially disastrous. When a water bomber makes a run to pick up water, it skims the lake surface at speeds upwards of 120 kilometres per hour. The pilot must have at least a kilometre of open, unobstructed water.

"Once we make a commitment and start scooping, we can't

avoid anything," says Neil Ayers, a pilot with the Ontario Ministry of Natural Resources. "It's like driving a Mack truck down a highway. That airplane is going in one direction, and that's straight ahead."

Don't even think about what happens when several hundred tonnes of water-laden bomber T-bones a fibreglass Chris-Craft at 120 kph.

You'd think anyone with the mental capacity to pull a starter cord could figure out that drag racing water bombers is about as smart as juggling live grenades. But you'd be wrong. Several pilots this year have reported "coming within a few metres" of smashing into the fools.

If it was just a case of obliterating the idiot boater, I'd write it off as a demonstration of Darwinism in action, but there's every chance the pilot might get killed as well.

Events like this remind us that not everyone who takes their recreation in the wilderness does so with the consciousness of Grey Owl or Ernest Thompson Seton.

But there is such a thing as divine revenge. I'm reminded of the story I heard about a confrontation between a northern Ontario park official and a couple of hunters from Toronto. The Ministry of Natural Resources official came across these two in the bush, sitting around a blazing campfire. At the height of the forest fire season. He explained that all fires were banned. The hunters shrugged, threw a pail of water on the fire and waited for him to leave.

The next day the MNR guy came back, attracted by a plume of smoke. He asked the hunters once more to douse the fire.

Three times he had to visit the campsite; each time there was a fire burning. Exasperated, he called up his supervisor.

"Leave it with me," said the boss. "I'll make sure the fire's out."

And not too much later, the hunters looked up from their campfire to see a fully laden water bomber just over the tree-tops.

And coming right at them.

And Deer Shall Graze

Time for a little environmental quiz, folks: where in the world do you think you would find the world's highest concentration of peregrine falcons?

Now remember, the peregrine is a very *rara avis* indeed. They need high mountains and square kilometres of pristine wilderness. Wealthy Arab sheiks covet the elusive creatures, often paying tens of thousands of dollars for black market nestlings. In the years after World War II, their ranks were decimated by DDT, which weakened their egg shells. Many environmentalists predicted the peregrine was on its way out.

So where would you go to find the healthiest remaining stock of peregrines? The High Arctic, perhaps? Somewhere in the trackless wastes of deepest South America? Perhaps high in the Rockies near McBride?

Nope. You would go to Gotham. Deepest darkest downtown Manhattan. The New York City area is awash with peregrines. They streak through the concrete canyons of Wall Street. They perch on the window ledges of the Empire State Building. They knock down pigeons in the skyways around the MetLife Building and the Marine Parkway.

A nest in the girders of the Brooklyn Bridge recently disgorged two perfectly healthy peregrine chicks.

The peregrine comeback wasn't entirely an act of God.

Humans helped. Biologists hand-reared peregrine chicks and eventually released them to "the wild." The transition to urban life was made easier by nesting boxes strategically placed in nooks and crannies of skyscrapers and bridges around New York.

Here in Canada, wildlife officials with Environment Canada were pleasantly shocked to discover a peregrine falcon nest on the top of an office tower deep in the bowels of Hogtown—less than a stone's throw from the intersection of King and Yonge streets.

"This is the first time in over fifty years that peregrines have nested in southern Ontario," one official said.

We shouldn't really be all that surprised. If there's one lesson that we pink, two-legged, mostly hairless creatures should have learned by now, it's the near-endless ability of our fellow earthly inhabitants to adapt to the depredations we visit on this planet.

Take raccoons. Take coyotes. Take the Canada Goose. Years ago all these creatures were associated with wilderness, or at the very least, rural living. Nowadays you can see raccoons dumpster diving in the downtowns of most of our cities. Coyotes are moving into the suburbs and casting covetous eyes at Fido's dog dish.

And the Canada Goose? I can remember when the news of a flight of Canada Geese would bring people piling out of the house, craning their necks skyward for a glimpse of the legendary vee. Today they stop traffic on Toronto's Lakeshore Boulevard and make a round of golf as hazardous as negotiating a minefield.

We're getting new species too. Who ever heard of zebra mussels a generation ago? Today by the billions they besmirch boat hulls and foul intake pipes from Cornwall to Kaministiquia.

And watch for something called the round goby. It's a fish, a tiny European import that showed up for the first time in Great Lakes waters recently. Some doomsayers predict it will make the zebra mussel look like a mild heat rash.

We should never forget the cardinal rule of life: Nature bats last. I'm reminded of something Timothy Leary once said at a press conference in England. Leary peered into his chemical crystal ball and predicted, "Deer shall graze on Charing Cross Road."

Well, sure, he was probably on drugs, but there was something arresting about the prophecy. The idea of deer daintily tip-toeing across a major intersection in London, England, plucking on the grasses growing up between the cracks in the pavement.

Deer shall graze on Charing Cross Road.

Leary didn't say anything about people being there.

Puppy Love

I have a new dog. If that statement causes you to yawn, blanch, retch or recoil in horror, turn the page now. For this is a dog story.

First a few words about my old dog, Rufus. He was a funny and faithful companion through three homes, two provinces and fifteen years before his legs gave out and he began to bark at groundhogs that weren't there.

When Rufus finally went to The Celestial Doghouse, we vowed never to have a dog again. Too much commitment, too much hair on the chesterfield, too devastating when they go and too expensive (did I mention Rufus was the recipient of two, count 'em, two root canals?).

We went muttless for a year and a half, right up until that fateful day we were driving into town and came upon two dogs doing . . . what pairs of dogs have an uncanny knack for doing in public at the most inappropriate times—usually when you're walking with your kids or chatting with the parson.

I don't wish to get graphic about what they were up to. Suffice to say that whatever they were doing, they were doing it doggy-style. The canine rampant was a beautiful golden retriever. Receiving his pitch, as it were, was an equally gorgeous black and white border collie.

My boon companion and I sat up as if cattle-prodded and

spoke with one voice. Right out loud. Right there in the car. And what we both said in perfect two-part harmony was, "We want one of their pups!"

A pup with the languid disposition of a golden retriever *and* the intelligence and trainability of a border collie? This is better than cloning! Besides, lots of folks get to see the birth of their puppies—how many get to be there at the conception?

To make a long and somewhat embarrassing story short, we stalked those two lovers like a pair of bloodhounds. We tracked them down a driveway and found out where the female lived. We confronted her owner, ascertained that his wayward girl was named Katy, informed him of the libidinous goings-on going on behind his back down by the road, and promised him a bottle of Scotch if we could have the pick of the eventual litter, if any.

The bottle of Scotch was delivered in late August, right after nine chubby balls of fur were also delivered by Katy, the winsome but decidedly tartish border collie. As I write, the pick of the litter (well, *our* pick; we chose her because she's kind of goofy) lies sleeping on my feet, exhausted from a day of digging in the flower beds, chewing slippers and peeing on the rug.

The haggard parents are just emerging from the "what the hell were we thinking" stage of dog ownership. We live in a welter of chew toys, rubber bones, rawhide knots and other assorted (and expensive) new dog paraphernalia, most of it in mint condition.

The boxes the toys came in, however, have been chewed pretty much beyond recognition. The dog thrives on paper, especially toilet paper. Amazing how many rooms you can canter through with a mouthful of Charmin Three-Ply before it's all unravelled.

Her name? Well, given her penchant for paper products, we were thinking of calling her MacMillan Bloedel, but we named her Woolly instead.

Which is almost as stupid. We don't even know how to spell it. Is it Woolly or Wooly? Or Woollie? Or Woolley?

Doesn't matter. Every time we tell somebody her name, they smile and pat her and say, "Good dog, Woody!"

Oh, yeah. About the divine mix of breeds? It's early days yet, but it looks pretty much like Woolly's got the brute strength and gargantuan appetite of the golden retriever plus the frenzied hyperneurosis of the Type A border collie.

I gotta go. She just peed on the rug again.

Bearing the Facts

I once had a teacher who told us, tongue wedged firmly in cheek, that all generalizations are for idiots.

She was probably right, but I'm going to risk one anyway: anybody who hunts bears is a dork.

I'm talking about those brave wilderness warriors who charcoal their cheekbones, don Desert Storm style camouflage fatigues, climb into their Jeeps and Jimmys and point the hood ornaments towards bear country. When they get there, they pick a likely looking spot, load their rifles and put out the bait. The bait varies, but it's never anything you'd want to see on the breakfast table. Sometimes it's a pail of ripe fish heads or a bag of putrefying garbage. The great white hunters park their lard butts within easy firing range of the bait and wait for a bear to show up.

The bears often do. Bears aren't too bright, and they'll eat just about anything, the stinkier the better.

And since it presents the profile of an upholstered dumpster, the bear is pathetically easy to shoot. Especially when it's got its head stuffed into a garbage can. It's about as challenging as hunting garden slugs with a hammer or fishing with grenades.

The question is, what kind of spiritual bankrupt could possibly consider bear-baiting a sportsmanlike experience?

Answer: a dork.

Or a poacher. Bear poachers make even the dorks look good.

Bear poachers kill bears any way they can—leg traps, poison, jack-lighting—and then they cut off their paws, hack out their gall bladders and leave the carcass to rot where it fell. Poachers know that there are sickos in the Orient who will pony up more than a thousand US dollars for a single bear paw—five grand US for the gall bladder—in order to concoct health potions. They also know their chances of getting caught by budget-strapped government forestry agents are slim.

Poachers are undeniably scum-sucking vermin, but at least they have a reason for slaughtering bears—they do it for the money, just like sneak thieves and hookers.

But the dorks? The so-called sports hunters? They do it for . . .
. . . the thrill?

They must be beginning to feel a little lonely. British Columbia has more bears than any other province, so many that it's legal to kill five thousand black bears alone each year. That probably means that British Columbia has more bear hunters as well. But that doesn't make hunting popular. A recent Angus Reid poll showed that nearly eighty percent of British Columbians are opposed to sport- and trophy-hunting of bears.

Not surprisingly, the dorks are trying to change the public image of their grisly addiction. A spokesperson for the US National Rifle Association argued in a recent press release that setting out bait for the purpose of blowing bears' brains out is actually . . . quite humane. The NRA reasoning—reasoning?—goes that baiting lets hunters get close enough to be sure that the bear they see in their crosshairs is not a sow with cubs.

Unless of course the sow has stashed her cubs in the bushes while she investigates, something sows with cubs usually do.

There is a simple way that all bear-hunting dorks could avoid shooting mother bears and orphaning cubs. They could give up buying barrels of fish guts and rancid horsemeat. They could donate their fantasy-stud, pseudomilitary hunting gear to the local theatre society or a costume shop. They could get smart, get serious, get on board, get with it.

They could get a life.

A Fewmet by Any Other Name

Birds do it . . . bees do it . . . even educated fleas
do it . . .

—Cole Porter

When deer produce 'em, they're called fewmets. When they come from otters they're called spraints. For dogs, the proper word is scumber, and for seabirds, guano. Even paleontologists have a special name for them. When they find samples produced by a dinosaur and fossilized by the ages, they call them coprolites.

I am referring, in case you haven't guessed, to poop.

Considering its commonality to all species, doo-doo doesn't get nearly the respect it deserves. Some species almost don't do it at all. The Guatemalan jumping viper hits the outhouse but once a month, while the average rabbit unloads about every three minutes.

Humans? Well, as you and I and the folks who make Exlax and the folks who make Kaopectate know only too well—it depends. If it makes you feel better, Sigmund Freud was constipated for the better part of his life, which probably explains that pained expression he wore. Good job Freud wasn't Italian. Mussolini was deeply suspicious of constipation. He considered it a symptom of latent communism, and ladled out copious doses of castor oil to anyone he considered a "carrier."

Other famous figures have ascribed great powers to common poop. The philosopher Pliny prescribed hippopotamus droppings as a cure for epilepsy. (Used in a poultice? Ingested? Do we really want to know?) Michelangelo slathered donkey dung on his statues to give them that aged look. Hippocrates swore by pigeon poop scalp massages as an antidote to baldness.

I have known hairlessness and I have known pigeon droppings. I believe I'd rather be bald.

Aside from quack remedies, has the stuff ever done us any good? You bet. Natives on our prairies depended on "buffalo chips" for fuel. For centuries China has used human excreta extensively for fertilizer. And some say that Australians never would have had organized agriculture if they hadn't imported millions of tonnes of guano to make their soil fertile.

Unidentified droppings have had their moment in the military side of world affairs as well. Back in the late seventies, when the United States was mired in a particularly deep swamp of doo-doo called the Vietnam War, newscasts and newspapers were suddenly full of speculation that the wily Viet Cong were launching chemical warfare attacks. The proof? Huge swathes of southeast Asian jungle foliage spattered with little yellow spots. It showed up on tanks and tents and even soldiers' helmets. US military advisors announced that it was "yellow rain," possibly a virulent, contagious form of deliberately spread chemicals and a complete violation of the Geneva Convention.

Actually it was bee poop. At the height of the monsoon season, bees in some parts of the tropics take wing in vast swarms, soar towards the heavens and engage (for reasons known only to bees) in a ritual of mass defecation.

Some interpreted it as a hymenopterous commentary on the stupidity of warfare, but whatever the cause, there was an alarming amount of bee guano about.

Which brings up the fascinating concept of volume. Some tiny microbes don't produce enough to register on a microscope slide, while the blue whale offloads up to three tonnes daily. On the plains of Serengeti in Africa, it's estimated that wildebeest herds leave behind four thousand tonnes of personal calling cards.

Per day.

Speaking of volume, let's have a moment of silence for the German zookeeper who, just a while back, lost his life in the elephant enclosure of a zoo in southern Germany.

Seems the chap had just finished administering a laxative to a badly constipated bull elephant. Then he made the fatal mistake of walking around the stern of the beast at precisely the moment that the laxative . . . took effect. Death was attributed to a combination of shock, asphyxiation and full-body trauma.

Of all the times to be caught without an umbrella.

Birds on the Brain

I have a confession to make. The time has come for me to come out of the closet. It's my duty to alert my faithful readers as to my true nature. I've already told my family. I've tried to explain it to the few friends I have left. I can only hope that our relationship can, however battered, survive based on a platform of mutual respect untainted by the poison of judgmental prejudices.

But I'm not sure it can. Not after I tell you that I am a practising . . .

Birdwatcher.

It's true. I realize now, looking back, that I have always been a birdwatcher, albeit a furtive one. As a kid I sucked in my breath as I watched the aerial antics of barn swallows and bats. I marvelled at the impossibly elegant, gravity-defying nests of orioles. Thrilled to the explosive thunder of a ruffed grouse taking flight from cover just centimetres ahead of my hiking boots . . .

I was watching birds, sure, but I wasn't a—you know—birdwatcher per se. I was still normal. Not one of those goofy fanatics you see in tennis shoes and Tilley hats, creeping through the raspberry canes with a *Peterson Field Guide* in one hand and a pair of Bushnell 7x50s in the other.

True, some of my most vibrant memories seemed to revolve around birds. I remember the otherworldly experience of hiking out on a cliff high on the Niagara Escarpment in southern

Ontario and seeing a pair of turkey vultures soaring at eye level, so close that I could see their beady little eyes and red neck wattles.

I remember sitting on a beach on the Caribbean island of Antigua, tracking white pelicans as they circled lazily high in the sky only to suddenly hurl themselves into steep, kamikaze dives right into the ocean.

They hit the surface with such force it didn't seem possible for them to survive. They did, and surfaced with a crawful of fish more often than not.

My favourite sight: arrowheads of Canada geese etched on a spring sky. My favourite sound: the eerie ululations of an unseen loon at dusk. My favourite smell: roast turkey on Thanksgiv—

Okay, a little cruel, but you get my point. One way or another, I've been birdwatching for years.

And then, a few years back, I moved to the West Coast. We get most of the regulars out here: robins, chickadees, starlings and crows. But there are also bald eagles and great blue herons, Steller's jays and rufous-sided towhees. Not to mention eight dozen different kinds of seagulls, none of which I'd ever seen before.

I've arrived in Birdwatcher Heaven. That's why I decided the time has come to out myself.

Mind you, I plan to take it one step at a time. I wouldn't want to make the blunder of British birdwatcher Neil Symmons. Mr. Symmons managed to attract a tawny owl to his garden. This was no mean feat, considering that he lives in downtown London and tawny owls are notoriously shy. Nonetheless, each evening for twelve straight months, Mr. Symmons has gone into his garden at dusk and called his owl. And each night for twelve straight months he's heard the unearthly, unmistakable hoot of a tawny owl answering him.

Symmons's wife Kim was so proud of Neil. She mentioned his evening pastime to her next-door neighbour.

"That's odd," said the neighbour, "my husband Fred spends his evenings out back talking to an owl . . ."

You guessed it. The two enthusiasts had been hooting to each other every night for a year.

Birdwatching. No one ever said it would be easy.

Glued to a Moment in Time

It was late on a winter evening, and I was prowling through the darkened bush, weapon in hand, searching for the biggest of all big game—an African lion.

Well, it wasn't that melodramatic. This bush was full of huge, quarter-hectare animal enclosures; my weapon was a Sony tape recorder and my guide was Brian Keating, education curator of the Calgary Zoo that we were prowling through.

We were trying to capture animal sounds that we could use in a radio program about the zoo. Brian figured there was a pretty good chance the resident lion would roar for us, if we were patient.

We found the lion enclosure. The male lion, a bleary-eyed old feller with a Bob Marley hairdo, was lolling just behind the wire mesh fence, sound asleep. He opened one eye at our approach, found us neither edible nor significant, and closed it.

Five minutes. Ten minutes. Not a movement. We stood there, me holding out a microphone like a lollipop bribe, the lion snoring.

Fifteen minutes. I turned to Brian and said, "Look, Brian this isn't going to w—"

And that's when my brain melted and the bottom dropped out of my stomach.

The lion had somehow, in the space of a nanosecond, gone

from flat out sleeping to full four-legged alert. He had also let out a—well, my tape recorder later confirmed that it was a "roar," but it was a roar I never heard.

I felt it. I felt like I'd shaken hands with a fifty-thousand-volt live wire.

Was I scared? Hell, yes. As scared as I've ever been—but I didn't run. I stood my ground. I had to. I was paralyzed.

But for a three-metre high wire mesh fence, I would have been an hors d'oeuvre that night. This happened to me about ten years ago, and I've never gotten over how utterly helpless I felt when that lion stoned me cold.

At least not until I read an article about some animal behaviour researchers at the Fauna Communication Research Institute in North Carolina. They've been studying tigers and they've discovered that the modus operandi of the beast is what they call "infrasound manipulation." They've determined that the tiger emits a low-pitched growl so deep that human beings can't even hear it.

But they feel it. And so does whatever the tiger is planning to put on the dinner menu that evening. The tiger mixes these infrasound growls with the roar that we do hear and the result is temporary paralysis, even among experienced trainers who've worked with the cats for years.

"It's an incredible force coming at you," says a Fauna Research spokesperson. "When they roar, tigers often move at great speed from lying down to straight up. During that time, you never have any thoughts of running away because you're so glued to the moment in time."

I believe it, because I know a mangy old African lion in the Calgary Zoo that can sing the same tune.

It's a tune you don't want to hear, even if you could.

Celebrity Bears

The bear—a big, skinny cub, really—was exhausted. It had been chased by the dogs for a whole, hot, miserable Mississippi afternoon, ending up trapped in a muddy waterhole, hounds on all sides of it, snarling and snapping.

One of the hunters galloped up, dismounted, leapt into the waterhole and clubbed the bear senseless with his rifle butt. The bear, alive but stunned, was hauled out and lashed to a tree just as the rest of the hunting party arrived on horseback.

"There's your bear, Mr. President," brayed the Great White Hunter who had clubbed it. "Go ahead, shoot 'im."

The year was 1902, and the man he was talking to was Theodore Roosevelt, twenty-sixth President of the United States. Roosevelt was an avid, even fanatical, hunter but he had his limits. A groggy, half-starved bear cub tied to a tree with ropes? That's where he drew the line. The president refused to shoot the bear. He also refused to let anyone else shoot it.

It turned out to be the best public relations decision Theodore Roosevelt ever made.

A sketch artist for the *Washington Post* had accompanied the hunting party and decided to immortalize the moment in a cartoon entitled "Drawing The Line in Mississippi." For some reason, the cartoon caught the public's fancy. And not just in the

Excited States of America; it went around the world and made Roosevelt famous as "a man of humanitarian principle."

It also gave birth to a children's fad that is as popular today as it was a century ago: stuffed bears. Our parents had them. You and I had them. Our kids have them. And we call them teddy bears because of that loveable old bear-sparer Teddy Roosevelt.

It's an odd coincidence, but just twelve years after the Mississippi encounter, a Canadian bear was about to step onto the world stage. The year was 1914, and a troop train had stopped in White River, Ontario, to take on water. A Canadian army lieutenant by the name of Harry Colebourn stepped off the train to stretch his legs. Down the platform he saw a grizzled old trapper with a bundle of black fur in his arms.

"What's that?" he asked.

The trapper held it out and said, "It's yours for twenty dollars."

It was a tiny black bear cub.

Lt. Colebourn bought the bear cub, dubbed it Winnipeg after his home town, and smuggled it aboard the train and later aboard the steamer that took the Second Canadian Infantry Brigade to England. The bear became the brigade mascot. He also grew rather sleek and fat from an excess of army rations.

When Lt. Colebourn got his marching orders to the French front, he left Winnipeg in the care of the London Zoo.

By now the bear's name had been shortened to Winnie.

And it was at the London Zoo that a British writer by the name of A.A. Milne and his young son Christopher first saw Winnie. Christopher loved the bear, so much so that his father began writing bear stories to entertain his son.

Those stories would soon become famous in dozens of languages around the world as *Winnie-The-Pooh*.

Winnie was back in the news recently when a painting of Pooh Bear, by the original illustrator of the books, sold at auction at Sotheby's for $243,000.

Quite an auspicious run for the little orphaned bear cub from White River, Ontario.

More auspicious than the run of the Mississippi bear that President Roosevelt so magnanimously declined to shoot back in 1902.

Actually Roosevelt wasn't quite the humanitarian he came to be portrayed as. True, he didn't shoot the bear tied to the tree. He walked away, muttering to an aide, "Put it out of its misery."

Which the aide did. With a hunting knife.

The *Washington Post* cartoonist didn't draw that part of the story.

Give Me Spots on Apples

There are some things I never expect to figure out: Why does the coffee in Prairie restaurants always taste so bad? How come Torontonians believe "the North" begins at Barrie?

And how come the Delicious isn't?

Delicious, I mean. The apple. You know the one I'm talking about. The bright red hand grenade with the little boobies on the bottom. Red as Madonna's lipstick; shiny as a Mountie's boot.

And tasteless as a mouthful of pages from the telephone book.

Believe it or not, they actually planned it that way.

There was a time when the Delicious apple really was delicious. You have to go back 130-odd years to 1872, when a farmer in Iowa crossed a couple of apple types and came up with a fire-engine-red, slightly elongated apple that no one had seen before. At a fall fair that year, the judge took one bite and bestowed a name on the new fruit that would stick for good.

"MMMmmmm," said the judge. "Delicious!"

And it stayed that way for the next eight decades or so, until somebody decided they could make the Red Delicious even better. The supermarket chains were demanding an apple with more eye appeal, better packing qualities and a longer shelf life. The apple growers experimented and came up with a thicker-skinned, shinier, more conical fruit.

The new product resisted bruising, could be stored for up to a year and was cosmetically perfect, just what the supermarkets ordered. Unfortunately it was also next to tasteless.

"Nobody should feel sorry for us," says Doyle Fleming, an orchard owner in Washington. "For almost fifty years we've been cramming down the consumer's throat . . . a product that was bred for colour and size and not for taste."

The sad truth is, we've been "dumbing down" apples for longer than most of us have been alive.

We all know Delicious, McIntosh, Spys and Spartans, but how about White Astrachan, Hightop Sweet, Maiden's Blush, Red Cheek Pippin, Yellow Transparent and Western Beauty? All varieties of apple that a hundred years ago you could buy by the barrel at the corner store. They're not extinct, but they're definitely on the endangered species list, and you'll never find them in the produce section of Loblaws or IGA.

There are something like eight thousand varieties of apple that we could be cultivating, buying and chomping into. But that would be inconvenient and cost-ineffective for the grocery tycoons, so we are left with five, maybe ten varieties to choose from.

There was once a fella from Brampton, Ontario, by the name of Bill Davis. He was the dullest, most uncharismatic *Homo sapiens* ever to strap on a necktie. He was also premier of the province for approximately two ice ages. When a reporter asked him the secret of his success, Davis almost broke into a smile and murmured, "Bland works."

Unfortunately it also works for apples, it seems, which is why you and I will likely never know the thrill of having the juice from a Hubbardson Nonesuch run down our chins. Not to mention a Roxbury Russet, a Newtown Spitzenburg or the magnificently monikered Westfield Seek-No-Further.

Or maybe I'm being unduly pessimistic. Some apple farmers are bucking the trend. They're going back to the old ways and the old days when producers didn't take their marching orders from some supermarket executive geek with a clip board and a fistful of flow charts. In Wisconsin, three hundred growers currently bypass the big American chains, selling directly to consumers. They're selling antique varieties and whole new strains of apples. Apples bred for—gasp!—good taste.

The same thing is happening in New York's Hudson Valley, where growers are marketing apples some of which don't even look like apples. They're putting out fruit that's striped or multicoloured. Apples that come in odd, nonstandardized sizes. Some even droop off the trees like pears.

There's a guy on the BC island I live on named Harry Burton. He grows 180 different varieties of apple on his farm and he does it without the use of herbicides, fungicides or pesticides.

Is it profitable for him? You bet your Sweet Winesap it is. Oh, I'm not sure if he's making a good living. But he looks to be making one helluva good life.

Look Up ... Way Up

I don't know how far ahead you book events in your date calendar, but if I were you, I wouldn't bother filling in any appointments beyond February 1, 2019.

Because that's the day the world ends. At 11:47 A.M. Eastern Standard Time, to be precise.

I know, I know—you're full of questions. Why so sudden? Why weren't you told earlier? How will this effect your RRSPs? Relax. Uncle Artie will explain all.

It's all the fault of a large chunk of rock that goes by the folksy moniker of 2002NT7. It's a rogue asteroid orbiting our sun once every 837 days. It is about the size of a small Prairie town. At 11:47 on that morning of February 1, just a few years from now, calculations indicate that NT7, as it is familiarly known, should be crashing through the earth's atmosphere at a speed of twenty-four kilometres a second. Depending on where it hits, it could create the greatest tidal wave of all time or wipe out a continent, throwing up enough dust to block the light of the sun for several months or even years.

And that doesn't just mean lousy tans for beach-goers—the world's food supply will be drastically affected. Crops will fail; trees and plants will wither and die. Nuclear winter will be upon us.

The last time this happened, the earth was populated by

dinosaurs. One day a couple of old Brontiess looked up from their salad brunches and noticed a speck in the sky that seemed to be getting bigger.

That particular asteroid was about the size of Saskatoon. It smashed into the earth just off the Yucatan peninsula and wiped out nearly seventy percent of all living species on the planet, including the dinosaurs.

Don't remember the fireworks? No surprise. It happened sixty-five million years ago.

Yet we've been bombarded from space constantly, before and since. It's funny how little attention we pay to stuff falling on us from outer space, considering we get about two hundred tonnes of celestial debris every day. Granted, most of it is just dust, galactic ice and tiny meteorites too small to even register, but every once in a while a lustier intergalactic gatecrasher barges in. Scientists estimate that, every century or so, the earth takes a hit from an asteroid about the size of a backyard swimming pool. And approximately every 300,000 years we play host to an asteroid the size of, oh, say 2002NT7.

The bad news is: we're overdue. The good news is: it almost certainly won't happen on February 1, 2019. At the moment, it looks as if NT7 could be on a collision course with planet Earth, but that's the case with dozens of potentially dangerous asteroids every year. As astronomers replot the orbits and refine their calculations, the odds against a head-on smackdown begin to lengthen. Dr. Benjamin Peiser of Liverpool John Moores University studies asteroids for a living. He has declared NT7 a mere flash in the pan.

"In all likelihood, in a couple of months additional observations will eliminate [NT7] from the list of potential impacts," he says. "I am very confident that . . . it is actually not on a collision course with Earth."

Which is good to know, for those of us who plan to be around just a few years from now. Still, if not then, when? And how much warning will we have? After all, these experts didn't even know that NT7 existed just a few short weeks ago. You have to wonder what else is lurking out there that they haven't noticed yet.

Such as G34.3.

This is a giant gas cloud currently bumping around in the Aquila constellation and identified by three British astronomers just last year.

How giant? Would you believe a thousand times larger than our own solar system? That's the big news. The even bigger news is: scientists have determined that this humungous gas cloud consists entirely of ethyl alcohol.

Enough ethyl alcohol that, were it bottled, they say, would result in four hundred trillion, trillion pints of beer.

Why, that's enough to fuel three, even four, Grey Cup weekends.

I hate to be a fatalist, but if we have to be hit by something from outer space, I know which intruder I'd choose.

Forget Armageddon—it's Miller Time.

Snowball the Dog

This is a story about a dog. A dog that belonged to a friend of mine in Thunder Bay some moons ago. A story I'm sure my friend would prefer to see buried deeper than a dog bone for all time. I have no wish to drag my friend or his canine into the limelight unnecessarily. So I'll just call him . . . Jim.

Hyder.

Jim thought it would be grand to get his little six-year-old daughter a puppy for Christmas. He thought it would be even grander if he took her with him to the Thunder Bay animal shelter so that she could pick out the pup herself.

With the benefit of hindsight, I'm sure Jim would agree that that was his first major blunder.

"I want the white one," chirped Laura. "The one eating the cinder block."

They took the white one. Laura named it Snowball. According to the animal control officer it was a husky, though if I'd had to guess, I would have leaned toward albino wolverine. Snowball was a certified hellhound. Mike Tyson should have had Snowball. Snowball made pit bulls look like pantywaists.

Not that Snowball was vicious. Just strong willed. Accent on the strong.

Laura could never take Snowball for a walk on a leash— she'd have been dragged to her death. Hell, even when Jim took him he looked like a water skier behind a runaway cigarette boat.

And then there was Snowball's appetite. Snowball was basically a fur-covered black hole. He gnawed chair legs. He shredded throw rugs. He ate whole couch cushions. He gulped, for God's sake, a three-hundred-gram tin of goldfish food—tin and all. He horsed his way through mountains of dog kibble and, without missing a bite, continued to eat the plastic dish that held the dog kibble. Snowball ate like he'd never been fed. Which was a problem. Jim was a single parent with a steady job. He couldn't leave Snowball outside all day, not in a Thunder Bay winter. But neither could he give him free run of the place. Not if he didn't want to come home to a hovel that looked like a Bronx crack house after a raid. So what Jim did—he loaded Snowball's food bowl, filled his water dish and locked him in the bathroom for the day. What could a dog do in a bathroom, eat the tub?

No. But he ate the toilet seat, demolished two towel bars and, Jim swears, scarfed half a dozen Bic razors.

One day Jim came home to find—it was springtime now—Snowball, who had been locked in the backyard, sitting happily with a powdery white moustache festooning his muzzle. Snowball had discovered, chewed open and devoured a bag of toxic rose dust—you know that poisonous stuff you put on rose bushes to kill bugs? Jim hurried to the shed to get the garden spade, hoping he could dig the hole, toss in the carcass and get the dirt tamped down before his daughter got home from school. Snowball just watched, snacking on the odd nugget of gravel Jim threw up. He didn't die from the poison. He didn't get sick. Jim swears that Snowball didn't so much as burp.

The dog was an indestructible, bottomless dynamo. When neighbourhood kids started throwing broken toys, plastic water bottles, even a two-metre fluorescent skipping rope into the backyard—laying bets on how long it would take Snowball to devour them—Jim knew the dog had to go.

He put an ad in the paper: "Free dog to a good home." Or maybe he didn't even specify good. The ad was answered by a

Little Old Lady. She, unaccountably, loved Snowball. The last Jim saw of the dog it was stampeding down the sidewalk, the Little Old Lady joined by the wrist, trailing out behind like a human streamer.

Another Jim—James Thurber—once wrote, "If I have any belief about immortality, it is that certain dogs I have known will go to Heaven. And very, very few persons."

Well, that's as may be. But if I ever get there and I spot a white dog cocking its leg against the Pearly Gates . . .

I'm gonna look St. Peter in the eye and say, "Cancel my reservation."

Playing with the Big Kids

Chances are if you ran into Phil and Roberta at a cocktail party or a barbecue, you wouldn't be particularly impressed. You'd think they were pretty average people and you'd be mostly right. They're in their forties, they run a graphic arts business from their comfortable two-storey house in upstate New York and they have a couple of youngsters, name of Casey and Charlie.

Middle-class, middle-aged and middle of the road.

Except for one thing. Those two youngsters? Casey and Charlie? They're girls.

And that's not all. They are also chimpanzees.

The older chimp—Charlie—came into Roberta's life three years ago when she heard Charlie's owner was going to sell her to a medical lab. Roberta gave her hubby Phil a nice candlelight and wine dinner that night. Over coffee she asked him how he'd feel about adoption.

Phil must have had a fair bit of wine. He said, "Why not?"

Two years later they realized that Charlie was suffering from lonesomeness. They tracked down Charlie's younger half-sister, Casey, at a private zoo in Missouri. Adopted her too.

How big a commitment is it, playing mom and dad to a pair of chimps? Very big. Most people don't know it, but cute and cuddly baby chimps grow up to be willful and pretty much unpredictable adults.

And very, very strong. At the age of only five, a chimpanzee can weigh more than a hundred kilograms. They have razor-sharp teeth and a vice-grip bite that can chomp right through a human arm. A single adult chimp has the body strength of five or six full-grown men. And when they hit adulthood, chimps don't move out and find an apartment of their own. Your average chimpanzee will live for fifty years.

Even as infants, chimps are more than a handful. They need nearly constant exercise and full-time attention too. Phil's and Roberta's house looks more like a jungle gym than something out of *Canadian House & Home.* The living room is festooned with ropes and swings. The furniture is all industrial-strength and indestructible.

And the humans haven't had a night off since they took in Charlie and Casey.

"You can't just hire a babysitter and expect them to be able to cope," says Roberta. "Chimps are very demanding—and they don't take to strangers."

Ironically Phil and Roberta have been taking heat from animal rights groups who give them a hard time for taking the animals out of their "natural" surroundings.

The animal rights folks don't appreciate that Charlie and Casey have never lived in the wild and that without Phil and Roberta both chimps would probably be languishing in some stainless steel medical lab providing statistical fodder for scientific experiments.

What's even more ironic is that Phil and Roberta agree in a way. "These creatures are really out of time and place," says Roberta. "[Their ancestors] should really have been left in the jungle. I feel bad that they don't have a real home."

Well, Casey and Charlie aren't faring badly under the circumstances. Roberta and Phil give them more love and attention than most human youngsters get.

And for what? Well, now, that's where it gets interesting. Because Casey and Charlie clearly give back something very real in the relationship they have with their two humans. You watch the four of them together and you become aware of a sense of wonder passing back and forth between the two species. The chimps are fascinated by the humans, and vice versa. There is a tangible bond of love shimmering in those great, moist chimpanzee eyes. And to watch the chimps hug and kiss—and, well, check their parents for fleas—is to see true familial affection in action.

And sometimes when you see Charlie pluck a ringing telephone off the wall and hold it to her ear or pour a cup of tea as neatly as your Aunt Winnie, or see Casey yawn and smack her lips and pull the covers over her shoulders as she drifts off to sleep just like any preschool child . . .

Sometimes you lose track of just who is chimp and who is *Homo sapiens*.

Leave It to Beaver

Just ran into a guy I know down at the coffee shop. He was handing out cigars.

"New baby?" I guessed cleverly.

"Yup," said the guy. "Eight-pound baby girl. We're calling her Charity."

Which would be fine, I guess, if the guy's last name didn't happen to be Case. Maybe the nurses will talk them out of it.

Mums and Dads . . . think long and hard before you saddle your newborns with monikers they have to carry for the rest of their lives. Keep it in mind that there are two Frank Zappa offspring who will, 'til they draw their last breath, answer to Moon Unit and Dweezil. Never forget that there's a university student in New York whose name is Rosetta Stone. And a chartered accountant in New Zealand named Genghis Cohen. And a Catholic Archbishop in Malta who answers to Cardinal Sin.

Names are like hand grenades. You never know when one is going to blow up in your face. Ask the folks at Beaver College down in Pennsylvania. It was an innocent enough name back in 1853, when the college was founded. And the institution came by the name honestly—the college was originally situated in Beaver County, Pennsylvania.

But the college has moved, and so have The Times. Tell someone you're going to Yale, Harvard, McGill or Simon Fraser and you get a little respect. Tell them you're studying at Beaver College and you get snickers, smirks and remarks like "You gotta be kiddin'!"

David Letterman has made fun of Beaver College on his *Late Show*. Howard Stern has mocked it on his radio program. Student Aimee Drumheller says it's hard to live with. She says when friends erupted in laughter at the mention of her alma mater, "I'd just kind of blow it off. But when they hear the name, they always want me to get them a Beaver College T-shirt."

For the beaver it's been a long, slow slide down the river bank. Back in the days before the big ships full of white strangers came, the beaver was plentiful—and a kind of living food bank for the Indians. They knew the creatures were fat, nutritious and easy to catch. The white men didn't give a damn about the meat. They just wanted the hides so they could send them back to Europe to be turned into high fashion headgear for style-conscious fops. And they took the hides by the millions. The beaver population plummeted close to extinction.

Fortunately European haute couture gave a flip of its frivolous head and poof! Beaver hats were suddenly out of fashion.

But fate wasn't finished with *Castor canadensis*. The poor little guy, through no fault of his own, became an involuntary charter member of vulgar slang.

Time was when our national emblem was just a shy and roly-poly rodent. Nowadays, as US linguist Reinhold Aman has noted, "When someone writes about beavers, one assumes this person is a zoologist, a Canadian, or works for a porn magazine."

Some critics say we never should have chosen a beaver for our national emblem, but let's face it, most of the blue-chip beasties were spoken for. Britain had the lion, Russia had the bear, India had the tiger. Our neighbours to the south had the magnificent bald eagle.

Magnificence, of course, is in the eye of the beholder. Listen to this description of the bald eagle:

"He is a bird of bad moral character . . . like those among

men who live by sharping and robbing, he is generally poor, and often very lousy."

I didn't say that. Benjamin Franklin did.

The late Robertson Davies opined that Canada should have chosen the Canadian lynx. "It is a daring, wily, beautiful animal, swift and potentially ferocious, tenacious in defence of what is its own and never caught asleep."

Bold attempt, Robertson—but try as I might, I can't picture Canada as daring, wily, ferocious or particularly swift.

And anyway what exactly is wrong with celebrating an animal that is quiet, hard-working, doesn't try to kill and eat its neighbours, minds its own business and spends its working hours building homes and creating new fish habitat?

Sounds like a pretty decent neighbour to me. Say it loud and say it proud: we come from beaver country.

Please Get Along, Little Dogie!

Remember *Rawhide*? Perhaps it was before your time. It was a TV western, really big back in the early sixties, all about a gaggle of cowboys who drove cattle across the West and the adventures that befell them in the doing of it. *Rawhide* was primarily notable as the debut vehicle for a lean, squinty-eyed newcomer by the name of Clint Eastwood.

The other thing that's remarkable about it is that, as a pro gram concept, *Rawhide* would never make it off the drawing board today.

Are you kidding? It was about cattle drives. The cowpokes in the show used to whoop and yell and wave their Stetsons and lasso stray calves and gallop after runaways. The theme song was a punchy, up-tempo ditty with lyrics that went, "Move 'em on, git 'em up, git 'em up, move 'em on, move 'em on, git 'em up, Rawhide (whip crack)."

Wrong, wrong, all wrong. Cowboys don't drive cattle any more. Not in this age of caring and empathy. The old and evil cattle drives have been replaced by "holistic herding." Also known as "low stress livestock management."

And how does that work exactly? Well, for starters, the Born Again Cowboys no long whoop and holler and gallop. Instead they coo and whisper and take extra care to make no sudden movements that might alarm or discomfit their four-footed charges. Instead of "driving" a steer in any given direction, the ex-cowboy-turned-relationship-counsellor gently moves into the steer's "space," then backs off when the steer moves toward him.

And the animals are never, ever approached from the rear.

You think I'm making this up, don't you? Well, I'm not. According to Steve Cote, a spokesperson for the US Natural Resources Conservation Service, "Low stress livestock handling is changing the whole face of the West."

I can see where if cattle had the votes, they'd poll solidly in favour of New Age Wrangling, but what's in it for the cowpokes?

"It's hard to believe at first," says Cote, "but the results are there for everyone to see—the cattle are happier, healthier and more obedient if they are not shouted at or subjected to stress. They tend to stay together and not wander away, and consequently life is easier for the cowboys."

Cote claims that the cattle will even accept being branded if they are talked to gently, which I find a little hard to believe. I've never actually had a piece of white-hot metal bearing a rancher's monogram slammed into my naked haunch, but I'm pretty sure no amount of sweet talk would persuade me that it was a good idea. If these sensitive New Age cowpunchers care about their cattle so much, why don't they deep-six the branding irons and break out the Magic Markers?

Still, holistic herding does look like an idea whose time has come. Predictably, a lot of the old ranch hands think it's so much longhorn puckie, but the men who pay their salaries are singing a different tune. Horace Smith is a rancher who runs a seventeen-thousand-hectare spread on the Nevada–Idaho border.

"It's not easy for a lot of [the cowboys]," says Smith, "but times are changing and they have to change with them."

"And," Smith adds bluntly, "if the cowboys don't want to change and do it our way then we don't want them."

Oh, I can see a lot of change heading due westward. Language alone is going to have to get a lot more sensitive. Perhaps cattle drovers will be issued with name tags that say "Hi, I'm Wilbur, your personal travel facilitator." "Cattle drives" could be renamed "ambulatory interspecies be-ins."

And what's to be done with those macho, decidedly uncool rodeos? Well, I suppose the calf roping portion could be redesignated as a series of rotating seminars on "Coping With Externally Imposed Restraints." The bucking bronco section might be overhauled and presented as "Equine applications of Newtonian Physics, or, What Goes Up Must Come Down."

All I know is, I'm glad John Wayne moseyed off to the Last Roundup before holistic herding rode into town. I don't think The Duke could have handled the whole dadburned concept.

But who knows? Maybe John Wayne had his sensitive side too. After all, his real name was Marion Morrison.

And I'm not making that up either.

Three Caws for Sammy

This is a message for Johnny Stutt. I don't know where he is or even *if* he still is, but if you happen to run into him, please let him know that I still remember what he did to Sammy.

Truth is, I haven't laid eyes on Johnny Stutt for close to half a century, back when we were both apple-cheeked, tow-headed grade schoolers walking back and forth to Humber Heights Public School. Johnny and I both lived on Braecrest Avenue.

Sammy? He lived at my place. I could almost always count on Sammy to be waiting at the corner of my driveway to caw me a "welcome home" at the end of the school day.

My dad had erected a signpost at the end of the driveway with our name and street number on it. Sammy liked to perch right on the top of the post, about three metres off the ground.

Which isn't so weird when you consider Sammy was a member of the *Corvus brachyrhynchos* family, which is to say, a common crow.

Well . . . not that common. No crows are. The term "bird-brain" does not apply to these rascally critters. Biologists have verified that crows can count accurately up to four and that they have a language of at least twenty-four different calls. Those calls include specific caw sequences that translate as "Come here," "Come back," "Feeding time," "Man with a gun" and "Let's get ready to rumble!"

What's more, crows mate for life and dote almost neurotically on their offspring, which often hang around the nest for as long as five years, helping to raise and look after subsequent broods.

Sammy didn't have those early life options. He was found at the bottom of a sugar maple—alone, wet and hungry—with no adults in sight. The kids who found him sold him to my dad, who brought him home in a cardboard box.

Sammy soon proved to be an uncommon common crow. He learned to speak a few words and, if you whistled for him, to come swooping in like a Harrier jet, landing on your shoulder with a delicacy that seemed at odds with his bulk. He also learned to retrieve nickels and dimes thrown in the long grass and to exchange them for a piece of fruit.

He must have imprinted strongly with his two-legged flightless adopters, because he grew to love people. Loved to watch them; loved to try and bum treats off them.

People didn't always return the friendship. Generally speaking, mankind seems to have an uneasy, mistrustful attitude toward the birds, and it shows in the language we use to describe them.

Correct name for a group of crows? A murder. Name for a crow fledgling? A simp.

If Sammy was aware that he was not universally adored by humans, he never let on. He continued to people watch at every opportunity. He was sitting atop his post watching the kids come home from school one day when Johnny Stutt came by and, for reasons unknown, chucked a rock at Sammy.

It hit him square in the chest. Sammy fell to the ground, thrashed himself upright and flew wobbling off. We never saw him again.

Anyone who's lost a pet knows what a void they leave when they go. It was even worse with Sammy. There's something about being the only kid on the block (maybe in the city) to have a personal friend who will sit on your shoulder, ride on your bike, go indoors and romp on the furniture, go outdoors and perform impromptu solo air shows over your head—there's something about that, once gone, that is irreplaceable.

I don't suppose I still carry a grudge for Johnny Stutt. Lord knows I made my share of stupid and cruel mistakes when I was a kid—still do, unfortunately. But there are those occasions when you wish you could rewind the Master Videotape of Life and edit out the rough spots.

Suppose I'd talked Johnny Stutt into playing catch that afternoon? Suppose I'd come home early and taken Sammy into the house or off in the fields?

I think that way about Sammy from time to time.

I like to think Johnny Stutt does too.

IV

|||

RULES OF THUMB

Hair Today and Gone Tomorrow

Just when I've decided that there is no new thing under the sun, my newspaper informs me that there's a brand new hair bank just opened down in California.

It's true, and you can make your personal deposit today. Just cut off a hank of your head hair and mail it to Mike Blaylock at Hairogenics Incorporated in San Francisco. Mike will (for a fee) take your truncated tress, custom-treat it to prevent disintegration, then vacuum-seal it in a protective baggie and ship it off to a fireproof, flood-proof, climate-controlled cellar vault in Portland, Oregon. There, your hair will stay until, well ... until something happens.

This isn't just a business venture for Mike Blaylock, it's a personal crusade as well. You see, Mike is one of millions of men who get a chilling message from their bathroom mirror every morning. The mirror tells them that they are slowly, inexorably succumbing to MPB, Male Pattern Baldness.

There are various tactics a man can adopt to combat Male Pattern Baldness.

He can slather goops and unguents like Rogaine into his retreating hairline.

He can shell out a small fortune to have plugs of hair yanked out of his back and punched into his scalp.

He can buy himself a hairpiece to replace the expanding divot on his skull.

There's just one downside to all these solutions. They don't work. The chemical treatments and the hair transplants will, at best, leave you with a head of hair that looks like a bad lawn. Hairpieces, aside from being uncomfortably hot and inherently treacherous, don't fool anybody. A man wearing a toupee invariably looks like he's transporting a small forest creature that crawled up on his head and expired.

Mike Blaylock figures there has to be a better way. He figures that science will inevitably come up with a genetic cure for baldness. Problem is, he might be bald by the time it happens.

Ergo the hair mausoleum in Portland, Oregon. The way Mike sees it, incipient baldies can store an actual sample of their hair until some future Dr. Frankenstein comes up with a procedure to take that preserved hair, revitalize it, and presto—a full head of hair once more.

Well, yeah, maybe, I suppose. But here's my advice, and I speak as a card-carrying chrome dome of three decades standing: Let it go, guys. It's no big deal.

What, after all, are the advantages of carrying a swatch of body fur over your eyebrows? Dandruff. A medicine cabinet crammed with expensive tubes and cans of mousse, gel, shampoo and conditioner. Greasy shirt collars. Regular trips to the barber to listen to stale hockey news and paranoid government theories.

Bald guys don't have to put up with any of that. We're like a paid-off house, free and clear. No overhead.

Besides, if you really, really want to save your hair there is one foolproof method. Go this route and I guarantee that not only will you go to your grave with a thick thatch on your noggin, you'll also be able to hit those really high notes like Céline Dion.

That's right, men, I'm talking about castration. There is no such thing as a bald eunuch. Put . . . well, baldly, a defoliating chap can elect to retain his testicles or his head hair, but not both.

So, ironically enough, baldness is a sign of virility.

Not everyone recognizes that. Some guys who are going bald fear that women will no longer be interested in them as partners.

Wrong, guys. Certain women may look down on hirsutely challenged suitors, but those are the airheads. Once they're out of your life you're left with real women with functioning brains, the ones who know that a cascading pompadour is about as important as, well, big boobs.

I say, skinheads of the world, unite. We obviously have nothing to hide.

Now if you'll excuse me, I think I'll slip out the back way.

Anything to escape those hordes of women hammering at the front door.

Bean There

As near as anyone can figure, it's all the fault of an Ethiopian goatherd by the name of Kaldi who watched over his flocks about 1,150 years ago. Each day Kaldi took his goats out to pasture. Then Kaldi got to squat on his haunches all day looking out for wolves.

Kaldi had a lot of time on his hands and not much to do, what with books not being invented yet and *Larry King Live* still almost a millennium away. Kaldi reached for a nearby plant and plucked some berries off a branch. He popped them in his mouth and began to chew.

Ka-bam! Kaldi felt a jolt. His heart began to hammer. His eyes grew wide as drink coasters. He felt good!

Kaldi had discovered coffee.

Okay . . . coffee beans. They weren't roasted, smoked or percolated, but they did the trick. Kaldi spread the word and for the next four hundred years or so, people in the Near and Middle East got their wake-up calls by chewing coffee beans.

Around about 1300 AD somebody accidentally dropped some coffee beans in a pot of boiling water, liked the smell and sipped the resultant brew. Ka-bam! Coffee tasted even better when it was boiled! For the next five hundred years or so, people drank their coffee instead of eating it.

But it was still pretty bitter. That lasted until yet another pioneer discovered that you could take the edge off boiled coffee by straining it through a jerkin, a dirndl, a saddle blanket or any other piece of cloth that happened to be hanging around.

By 1800, coffee was getting almost pleasant.

We have come a long way since then. If you ever doubt it, take a stroll down the streets of Vancouver and let your head swivel from side to side, counting the coffee shops that abound.

Vancouver is coffee crazy.

You can't just go into a Vancouver coffee shop and order a cup of java. No, you have to choose from espressos, lattes, mochas, cappuccinos. Then you have to specify if you want a small, medium or grande.

And will that be with skim, two percent, homo or whipped cream?

It gets more complicated. Caffeine addicts can now opt for something called the Frappuccino. What's in it? Search me. I hear that it's ice-cold, contains only three hundred calories and looks something like a Slurpee.

One thing you can count on—it's packed with caffeine.

I'm waiting for the first shipment of something called Kopi Luwak coffee. This stuff sells, if you can believe it, for fifty US dollars a kilogram in San Francisco.

What's so special about Kopi Luwak coffee? Well, it has to do with the way that it's . . . processed.

You see, in Indonesia, where Kopi Luwak originates, there exists a small tree-dwelling marsupial called a paradoxurus that likes to feed on coffee beans.

Are you beginning to get the picture?

The paradoxurus eats the coffee beans, which it later excretes fairly intact. Then some poor slob has to poke through paradoxurus doo-doo gathering "processed" beans.

Makes you wonder if the human craze for coffee hasn't gone about as far as it can go.

Perhaps it has. Care to hear about the latest product of a Colorado conglomerate called Allegro Coffee?

Tea. Allegro is offering a whole new line of teas including

Earl Grey and orange pekoe knockoffs. The company is merely responding to a trend. In the past five years, tea sales in the United States have grown by almost seventeen percent.

"Tea is quieter than coffee," says an Allegro rep. "Tea is a Sunday drive in the country. Coffee is Monday morning on the freeway."

Yeah. And you never know where those coffee beans have been.

Fashion Is Not My Long Suit

I've always had a problem with suits. Men's suits, I mean. The two-piece number, the jacket and trousers. Part of my problem is that I realized early on that most of the people likely to cause me grief in life would be wearing suits: the principal, my teachers, the bank manager, any lawyer. The suit was a metaphor for The Enemy. If I saw somebody in a suit I knew trouble was not far off and probably on the way.

Another part of my suit problem: I spent a fraction of my formative years in Morocco, where I came across the ultimate male garment. It is called the *djellaba* (spelling varies). It's a loose, hooded woollen cloak with full sleeves that cover the hands.

But the *djellaba* is so much more than a cloak. It is warm enough to protect you from the cold. It is also insulated to protect you from the heat. The deep hood will safeguard your privacy and anonymity. It is roomy, cozy and hardy. You could be naked in your *djellaba* or you could be dressed like the goalie for the Nashville Predators. No one could tell from the outside. It is a self-contained habitat. You can almost live in a *djellaba*. It is everything a North American business suit isn't.

The late, great Peter Gzowski—author, journalist, radio star, kamikaze TV host—once vowed that he would never again take a job if he couldn't wear jeans to the office. This was way back in the sixties, when, unless you were bruising your knuckles for a living, suits and ties were *de rigueur*.

Luckily for Gzowski, he was immediately hired by the CBC where dress codes are not just optional, they're unknown. (The CBC brass doesn't care if you wear a Batman cape or pasties and a thong; they're just happy if you show up for work.)

But I digress. The point is, as Gzowksi pointed out half a century ago, the business suit is one of the central absurdities of modern North American life. Why are so many of us still wearing this supremely inappropriate garment?

Think about it. A flimsy, two-piece outfit that can't keep you warm at a bus stop in February and will drive you to heat prostration at the same bus stop in August. It lacks the sturdiness of overalls, the comfort of a sweat suit and the stretch of spandex. What is the business suit good for?

Not much, and it's been out of date for decades. Ever wondered why men's suit jackets have a vent in the rear? For riding horseback. It was designed to drape over a saddle. When's the last time you saw a broker ambling down Bay Street on a cayuse?

The buttons on the sleeves? They were put there to dissuade British seamen from wiping their snotty noses while standing in assembly. What Limey sailors have to do with modern commercial dress is anybody's guess, but it makes as much sense as anything else about men's suits.

Suit jackets are awkward and cumbersome when you're climbing into the bucket seat of a Mazda Miata or cramming your limbs into an economy rathole on an Air Canada flight to Moose Jaw. They just get in the way, just as they do when you're working in a climate-controlled office. The jackets get slung over chairbacks. What's the point?

Men's suits should have gone out of vogue or morphed into something useful a hundred years ago, but for some reason they didn't. Women's fashion went through long gowns, medium gowns, flouncy gowns, flared waists, high shoulders, empire gowns, the sack, the maxi, the midi, the mini, the monokini. Men just kept wearing the same dumb suits. Oh, the lapels waxed and waned. The cuffs came and went. The trousers flared and shrivelled. But it was the same dumb suit underneath.

I've got half a mind to start a movement to recall the business suit and replace it with the *djellaba*, except . . .

Except I remember a conversation I had with a professor in Tangier a few decades ago. I was ranting, then as now, about the stupidity of the business suit and the superiority of the *djellaba* when he put a hand on my arm and asked if I had any theory on why North African culture had essentially stalled—made no progress—since virtually the middle ages. I said I'd never thought about it.

"The *djellaba*," he said. "It is the most comfortable garment for this climate imaginable. But the sleeves are heavy and long. You can't hammer nails when you're wearing it; you can't repair watches, or work machinery. It's hard to write or even read a book. It's comfortable all right. Problem is, it's too comfortable."

Hmm. Perhaps I won't take my business suits to the thrift shop just yet.

Immortality and the Arthur Fly

Immortality? A fate worse than death!

I don't think a lot of folks would agree with Edgar Shoaff, the man who penned the aforementioned sentiment. I think most people would give their left lung for the chance to live forever. We are not the least bit satisfied, swallowing the bitter knowledge that we are no more than flimsy moths around the candle flame of life. That's why we wear girdles, dye our hair, lather on wrinkle cream and make doctors rich by purchasing lip enhancements, boob lifts and bum tucks. We like to pretend to the rest of the world that we're utterly ageless.

Unfortunately, in the game of body alterations, there's only one rule: Gravity bats last. If you don't believe me, look at Nancy Reagan, Joan Rivers and the actress Eartha Kitt. They've all spent fortunes on plastic surgery. They all look like anorexic vampire bats.

There are other ways to chase immortality. Fame, for instance. But it's no lead pipe cinch either. I am sure, in their heydays, that Rudolph Valentino and Clara Bow thought they'd be household words forever. But a modern teenager wouldn't know if they were people or ice cream flavours.

Sometimes fate can be especially cruel. Your name becomes immortal but you are utterly forgotten. Do you know who Buick is? Or Chevrolet? How about the Amana who got all those freezers named after him? Or the Norden who invented the World War II bombsight?

Gone. Forgotten like umpteen hundred thousand Smiths and Joneses before them.

Fortunately there is a way to become immortal. And wouldn't you know it, Canadians are responsible for it. Canadian entomologists, as a matter of fact, in the employ of the University of Manitoba.

The U of M, like most nonprofit institutions trying to live through these austere times, is strapped for cash. But the university's department of entomology is not going to die without a whimper. It's fighting back.

By selling immortality.

It works like this: a bunch of the boys in the bug department were sitting around one day talking about what they could do to generate some cash flow. One of them mentioned that all they had in the way of assets was several hundred billion creepy crawly critters.

"And," added one of them ruefully, "nearly half of them haven't even been named yet."

Which is when the light bulb of opportunity went incandescent for the entomologists. Why not, they asked themselves, sell off insect labelling rights to well-heeled, immortality-seeking Canadians? Said Canuck customers would get to see their names live on in learned scientific journals, and the scientific community would pick up some very much needed cash.

"Most of these names last forever," says Robert Roughley, a spokesperson for the entomology department. Roughley also admits that the idea wasn't exactly original. The London Stock Exchange has been selling off names of bugs found in Costa Rica for more than a year now.

"Certainly it's been done in the past," admits Roughley, "But we think it's an idea whose time has come back."

How does it work? Dead simple. You, with Visa card in hand, call up the University of Manitoba Department of Entomology. They read you out a list of insects that are ready, willing and able to carry your name down the corridors of eternity.

Is it cheap? Depends on what you want. You can give your moniker to a lowly water beetle for as little as two hundred dollars. Of course if you're in the market for something a little fancier—a moth, say, or a katydid—well, that's going to cost you a little more.

And just to get the ball rolling, the folks in the U of M entomology department have named two hitherto anonymous insects after one of our former illustrious leaders. You won't be surprised to learn that among his many national depredations as prime minister Brian Mulroney slashed government funds for research and development, severely crippling work at universities right across the country, not least at the University of Manitoba.

Do the Manitoban academics bear a grudge? Hah! You underestimate the generosity of spirit to be found in the U of M's entomology department. Why, already they've named two bugs after the ex-PM, absolutely free.

One is the Mulroney insect, a near-sighted bug with a nasty bite. The other is the Meech Fly, a small winged creature that lives on dung and inhabits the Meech Lake area.

A spontaneous gesture of good will, the entomologists call it.

Typecasting, I call it.

Beauty Is Only Scalpel Deep

Consider the case of a gorgeous South American by the name of Juliana Borges, only twenty-two years old and by all accounts stunningly, supernaturally beautiful. So beautiful that she was chosen as Miss Brazil. There are 170 million people in Brazil and half of them are women. Juliana Borges has been judged the comeliest of them all.

And to what does this statuesque, willowy siren owe her great good fortune? To fabulous genes? A perfect diet? Pure, dumb luck?

Nope, nope and nope.

Miss Brazil owes her title to her personal plastic surgeon. In her twenty-two years on the planet, Miss Brazil has been under the knife no fewer than twenty-three times. She has plumped up her breasts with silicone. She has had fat vacuumed off her thighs. She has had her ears sculpted, her nose bobbed, her cheeks and jaws padded out with sundry inert materials and she has seen to it that various birthmark-type anomalies have been sandblasted to smithereens.

"Plastic surgery made me more beautiful," says Juliana. "It gave me the confidence in myself and the perfect measurements that won me this title."

It's a sad tune but not a new one. Pamela Anderson used plastic surgery to give herself a bustline like the prow of a Chris-

Craft. Joan Rivers, the wisecracking talk-show harpy, gleefully spent hundreds of thousands of dollars over the past few decades fending off Father Time by having herself nipped, tucked, padded, abraded and otherwise surgically shored up. To me she looks like an X-ray of the walking undead but she seems happy with the ersatz apparition she sees in the mirror each morning.

Whatever works, I guess. Juliana Borges, along with her resident silicone hummocks and blobs, represented her country at the Miss Universe pageant and nobody seemed to be unduly upset about it.

Call me old-fashioned, but I would have thought a contest dedicated to seeking out feminine pulchritude would have specified that it be natural, not plastic.

Funny things happen when people resort to self-sculpturing. Michael Jackson used to have a pretty normal-looking nose. Now, after umpteen rhinoplasties, he has little more than two blowholes in the middle of his face.

And then there's the case of the French performance artist who calls herself Orlan. Mademoiselle Orlan has recently completed the final stages of a ten-year work that she calls "The Reincarnation of St. Orlan."

What she had done is—and I wish I was making this up—she's had a team of plastic surgeons construct the largest nose her face can support *while she lectured on postmodern philosophical theory.*

Ah, beauty. Voltaire once said, "Ask a toad and he will tell you that beauty is a female with two great round eyes in a tiny head, a large flat mouth, a yellow belly and a brown spotted back."

I dunno. Next to Mlle. Orlan, that sounds pretty hot to me.

Coffee, Tea or None of the Above?

A nybody got work out there for an airplane captain? An ex-airplane captain, actually. Worked for Northwest Airlines for twenty-two years, right up until that fateful day last November when, sitting in the cockpit of his Boeing 727, waiting in line to take off from Las Vegas to Detroit—he finally cracked.

It was the inflight meal that did it. The stewardess brought two trays forward into the cockpit, one for the captain and the other for his copilot. The captain peeled back the tinfoil, took one look, hung up his earphones and got off the plane.

Not only got off the plane, but called for a taxi, took the taxi from the airport to a nearby restaurant, ordered a meal to go, and then taxied back to his plane. His passengers were not amused, and neither were his superiors, who sacked him for "conduct unbecoming," etc.

But that's gotta be the last word on airline food: so bad even the staff won't eat it.

Now it must be said that, next to dissing Revenue Canada and lawyers, dissing airline food is the cheapest laugh you can get. Everybody has a one-liner about those unidentifiable globs of gorp and goo they serve on planes.

Question: Why do they serve alcohol on airplanes?

Answer: So you won't mind the meal. Arf, arf.

Well, as Sam Goldwyn said, include me out. I happen to—
are you sitting down?—like airplane food.

When I'm flying from Vancouver to Sheep Butt, Wyoming,
and some smiling stranger is kind enough to offer me a complimentary meal, I say "Sure! You bet!" with tears of gratitude
welling up in my eyes. When the mystery tray comes I invariably
vacuum up every morsel in front of me. What's more, if the passenger next to me leaves that wedge of Styrofoam pie on his tray,
I ask for that too. For two reasons.

Number one: I'm not fussy. From a reserved banquette at a
five-star restaurant to a counter stool in a back-alley beanery, I
never met a meal I didn't like.

Number two: I eat the airplane meal out of respect for technology.

Are you kidding? I'm in a giant aluminum cigar tube, ten
thousand metres in the air, going six hundred kilometres an
hour over the Rockies, the temperature outside is minus forty,
I'm about to watch a movie *and* I get a hot meal for free? Of
course I take it.

Even if I can't tell what the main course is trying to be.

A hundred years ago the only way to get from Vancouver
to Wyoming was on foot, swatting at black flies and gnawing
on a chunk of frozen pemmican. I consider the preparation and
presentation of a cooked meal, complete with coffee and dessert,
eight kilometres straight up over Red Deer, Alberta, to be an act
of pure, unadulterated magic.

And it's only the beginning! Aeronautics is an industry that
grows in gallops. Yesterday, we were flying in propeller-driven
planes with canvas wings. Today we can fly across the Atlantic in
our shirtsleeves, sipping Bloody Marys and watching Brad Pitt.

As for the future? Hey, it can only get better! I can visualize
an aircraft about to take off a hundred years from now. Flight
attendants are long gone, replaced by cheery and efficient robots
that scuttle up and down the aisle.

The aircraft will be piloted by computers the sophistication
of which we can't begin to imagine. The flight will take off so

smoothly we won't even know we're in the air. Not until a comforting mechanical voice begs our attention and makes the standard inflight announcement: "Good evening, ladies and gentlemen, and welcome aboard GatesAir flight 1798. Our flying time to Rio de Janeiro will be precisely eleven minutes and twentynine seconds. In the meantime, relax and let our cyberstews cater to your every whim.

"And those of you who might be the slightest bit worried about flying with GatesAir (the world's first all-mechanical airline) can relax in peace, knowing that this flight is absolutely free from the possibility of human error. Every detail of the flight—altitude, cabin pressure, course corrections, takeoff and landing—is continuously monitored by state-of-the-art computer circuitry, providing you with a worry-free flight, secure in the knowledge that absolutely nothing can go wrong . . . go wrong . . . go wrong . . . "

To Make Your Heart Strings Crack

Ever wondered how many smells there are in the world? A lot more than you'll find in Mary Dobson's entertaining "scratch and sniff" history books. Scientists have classified more than seventeen thousand individual odours, and they're still sniffing. According to their data, the very worst whiffs you can encounter come from two chemical compounds: ethyl mercaptan (didn't she play in *I Love Lucy*?) and butyl seleno-mercaptan, both of which put out a stench the researchers say is "reminiscent of a combination of rotting cabbage, garlic, onions, burned toast and sewer gas."

Boy, when it comes to fun jobs, some folks have horseshoes up their lab coats.

Smells are a very personal thing. One man's meat is another man's *poisson* and all that. The poet Schiller kept a handful of rotting apples on his desk. Claimed the smell inspired him. On the other hand, the smell of a common hot dog made Ethel Barrymore throw up. Smells are even more personal than that. Some of us just smell more than others, and not just individually—collectively too. Research shows that we Caucasians have more BO than Orientals. In fact Dr. William Taylor, an olfactory expert, claims the Japanese invented the aerosol air freshener to fumigate rooms after a Westerner had passed through.

The scent of a certain lily is one of the nicest fragrances I've ever inhaled, but you wouldn't want to confuse it with a lily called *Rafflesia arnoldii*, which grows in the jungles of southeast Asia. Southeast Asians don't call it *Rafflesia arnoldii*. They call it the stinking corpse plant. Self-explanatory, I think.

Thankfully smells can be just as wonderful as they can be horrid. And familiar smells can whisk you back decades in a heartbeat. It's been years since I rode a horse but I know exactly what a horse's back smells like when you hoist the saddle off. Odours don't seem to age like other memories. I can still smell new-mown hay and the gamey reek of friction tape and male sweat and damp leather in a hockey dressing room. Who can't remember the smell of lilacs? The pungency of gasoline in an outboard motor? And if you're an ex-smoker, the aroma of your last cigarette?

My all-time favourite smell is one I haven't breathed in for quite a spell. It's the smell of a place. A restaurant in the basement of the Ontario Public Stockyards where I worked as a kid. It's a smell that combines cigarette smoke, fried onions, farmers boots with dried cow manure on 'em and hickory cattle canes, all seasoned with the smell of Heinz 57 Sauce—you know that kind of orangy steak sauce that comes in a bottle like a mickey?

Haven't smelled that smell for more than forty years. But I can sniff it in my mind like I had breakfast there this morning.

That's the beauty of smells. Rudyard Kipling said it all in a poem:

> *Smells are surer than sounds or sights*
> *To make your heart strings crack*
> *They start those awful voices o' nights*
> *That whisper, "Old man, come back!"*
> *That must be why the big things pass*
> *And the little things remain,*
> *Like the smell of the wattle by Lichtenberg*
> *Riding in, in the rain.*

Yeah. That, or the old Stockyards restaurant.

This Gland Is Your Gland

Is it my imagination, or are there really a lot more boobs in the news these days? Some days it feels like you can't turn around without being poked in the eye with yet another mammalian-oriented bulletin. Case in point: this snippet from a recent newspaper.

> OSLO, Norway (Reuters)—A bare-breasted blonde mermaid atop a rock is making tourists gape along a Norwegian fjord.

It seems a comely wench by the name of Line Oexnevad (would I make that up?) has taken it upon herself to personally recreate the legend of Denmark's Little Mermaid, but in the coastal waters of Norway. Accordingly Ms. Oexnevad, decked out in naught but a long blonde wig and a swishy neoprene fishtail, has shimmied herself up onto a picturesque rock along the Lysefjord at least a half dozen times over the past three summers, then lolled back and waited serenely for passengers aboard the tourist boats to notice.

They noticed.

"One man even jumped off a boat and swam over to me," she marvelled.

Yeah, well, it probably wasn't the neoprene fishtail, Line.

It's amazing, the power of a simple gland . . . or two. The island I live on recently went through a gangbanging by an off-shore logging company. Not surprisingly, that elicited a variety of protests from the people who had to live with the results. Logging roads were blocked, protestors chained themselves to logging equipment, placard-wavers marched on the legislature.

And none of these initiatives garnered one-tenth the attention that was lavished on a simple, black and white twelve-page calendar.

It's called "Salt Spring Island Women: Preserve and Protect."

Each month of the calendar featured various women of the island dressed in strategically placed lambs, spruce boughs, here a backpack, there a dulcimer—and very little else.

The calendar is not in the least salacious or pornographic—you'd see more flesh on the guest couch of the Letterman show any night of the week—but it is beautifully photographed and the subjects are . . . quite lovely in an unHollywood way. Lovely, and clearly unclothed.

And naturally the calendar sold like hotcakes. It was conceived as a modest fundraiser to protest the logging, but it turned into a runaway bestseller. They had inquiries and orders from every part of Canada, all over the States, even Europe and Asia.

Why? Chalk it up to the Boob Factor. Despite decades—centuries, even—of what should have been overexposure (think Lady Godiva, Winged Victory, Venus on the Half Shell, Sophia Loren, Xena the Warrior Princess) the simple human female breast still has the power to shock and. . . well, titillate.

Just another dumb male thing, you think? Not exclusively. Tommy's Bar and Grill in Maple Ridge, BC, ran a competition tastefully entitled the Win Boobs Contest. First prize: a three-thousand-dollar plastic surgery breast-enhancing operation.

Crass, offensive, sexist and an insult to womanhood, right?

Yeah, well, the folks at Tommy's had over two thousand entries in their ballot box—all from hopeful women.

Meanwhile, boob technology marches on. A company of British engineers named Ove Arup has announced a brand-new, state-of-the-art brassiere called Bioform, soon to be available at better lingerie stores everywhere. A press release claims the new bra is revolutionary. Seems they've replaced the underwire with plastic bands which they claim "more comfortably distribute the load and reduce stress."

Sounds. . . uplifting, until you learn that this is the same engineering firm that designed London's Millennium Bridge.

You know, the one that was closed to traffic because it was too . . . wobbly.

Ladies, you've been warned.

I'm Chewing as Slow as I Can!

Every meal I eat leaves me feeling like a loser. Not a weight loser, I eat way too much for that. I feel like a moral loser.

I start each meal with a firm resolve to follow the advice my public school nurse gave my class, lo those many decades ago.

"Chew each mouthful at least twenty times," Miss Patchett told us. "It's the key to a healthy digestive system."

I believed her. Still do. And each time I sit down to eat, whether it's a bowl of granola or a T-bone with a baked potato, I tell myself that this time, *this time*, I am for sure going to do the twenty times per mouthful thing.

Never happens. I always end up hoovering my plate clean in a feeding frenzy that would do a piranha proud.

And our beloved food manufacturers aren't making my speed-eating an easy jones to kick. I don't know if you noticed or not, but fast food is getting faster every day.

For folks who suffer from the twin afflictions of liking yogurt and being in a hurry, there is a product called Yoplait Gogurt. This is yogurt that you can squirt straight into your mouth from a tube.

Campbell's Soup has a new line they call Ready-To-Serve Classics. Forget about adding water and you can toss out your can opener to boot. With Ready-To-Serve Classics you just peel, nuke and slurp away.

And for you folks who want your morning breakfast but can't spare the time to actually sit down at a table and eat it, Breakaway Foods has just the product line for you. They call it IncrEdibles. It's a full range of all your favourite morning treats: scrambled eggs, macaroni and cheese, pancakes with syrup . . .

On a stick. Like a Popsicle.

Now you can microwave your IncrEdible, run to your car and join the morning rush hour traffic jam, eating with one hand and steering with the other. If they came up with a way to glue a cellphone to the other end of the stick, life would be complete.

And then there's PJ squares. If you're like me, a substantial part of your teenaged diet was peanut butter and jam sandwiches. A slice of bread, a slash of butter, a gob of peanut butter topped with jam. Fast food doesn't get much faster than that, right?

Wrong. You can now buy PJ squares. These are individually wrapped slices that have a thin strip of peanut butter on one side and a smear of jelly on the other. Just unwrap it, slap it on a slice of bread and lunch is made. Or if you're really desperate, forget the bread. Just roll up your PJ square like a limp taco and pop it in your mouth. Now *that's* fast food. It gives a whole new intensity to the term "eat and run."

And then there is the other end of the digestive spectrum: Slow Food. It's a movement that's already big in Europe (sixty-six thousand members strong) and beginning to catch on in North America.

The Slow Food movement was founded back in 1986 by a group of—surprise, surprise—Italian food lovers who got sick and tired of the expanding commercial juggernaut we call fast food outlets. Slow Food's whole premise: food isn't supposed to be fast. It's supposed to be leisurely and lovingly prepared and enjoyed. Eat and run? Forget it. Slow Food lovers believe a decent meal should take as long as an opera, a theatre production or a romantic rendezvous. They seek out and encourage restaurants that feature local recipes and cater to small, unhurried clienteles. Above all they want us all to relax and take a breather with our meals. Their symbol is a snail.

"Fast food is not genuine food," says a spokesperson. "It fills you up without sustaining you. I think people are tired of eating things that have no taste, no history, no link with the land. They want something better."

Sounds good to me. I haven't seen any restaurants with a snail logo on the menu, but I'll keep an eye out. In the meantime I'm going to practice. If you spot a guy in the local diner who's hunched over the blue plate special and looks like he's talking to himself, don't call the cops. It's only me, in training.

I'm chewing, Miss Patchett, I'm chewing.

Now I Lay Me . . .

*Sleep is the most moronic fraternity in the world,
with the heaviest dues and the crudest rituals.*
—Vladimir Nabokov

Methinks the author of *Lolita* doth protest too much. That sounds like something that might have been scribbled down in the early hours of some sleepless night by a grumpy insomniac fed up with counting sheep.

Still, he does have a point. Just imagine what a Type A personality could get done if said personality didn't have to render itself unconscious for one-third of its lifetime. Assuming that you, like me, hit the sack for about eight hours a night, and assuming that we both make it to our allotted three score and ten, that means that you and I will have spent close to a quarter of a century curled up and comatose in the Land of Nod.

Some folks have tried to stuff sleep on the back burner. Napoleon, Edison, Churchill and George Bernard Shaw all got by on less than five hours sleep a night, or so they claimed. Benjamin Franklin swore he slept only two. Einstein on the other hand, liked to rack up ten hours in the sack each night—eleven, if he had a major cogitation day coming up.

So how much sleep do we need? The jury is still out. Edison growled, "People eat twice too much and sleep twice too long." But Paul Martin (not him, the one who wrote the book *Counting Sheep*) says, "We might live longer and happier lives if we took our beds as seriously as our running shoes."

One thing that most experts agree on is that we are all getting less sleep than we used to. Blame television, electric lights, Internet surfing, Starbucks or just the sheer hyped-up pace of modern life. Whatever the cause, there are a lot of folks walking around with unclaimed luggage under their eyeballs.

And when it comes to the phenomenon of sleep, that may be just about all we can agree on. Most of our notions about sleep are erroneous. People talk of "sleeping the night through." In fact we get four or five "sleeps" of about ninety minutes each. People who claim they never dream are wrong. They just don't remember their dreams. And we talk of "sweet dreams." In fact about two-thirds of our dreams are unpleasant.

Scientists aren't even precisely sure why we need to curl up and pass out once a day. Some argue we sleep to restore the body. Others say we do it to conserve energy. Certain researchers claim the function of sleep is to allow the brain to process the day's experiences and file them away in the memory banks—to help us remember, in other words. Other researchers say the opposite: that sleep is like your computer's off switch. It prevents the brain from becoming overloaded.

As to how much sleep we need, that too is an open question. The health guides recommend eight hours a night, but there's a seventy-year-old woman in England who claims she's never slept more than one hour a night, and no daytime naps either. Researchers hied her off to a sleep lab and monitored the woman for seventy-two hours straight. She stayed awake for the first fifty-six hours (nearly two and a half days) and then slept for only an hour and a half. The records show the woman awoke refreshed, alert and in good spirits.

Well, why not? Sleep is not an absolute biological imperative. Albatrosses can fly for thirty to fifty days without resting. As far as we can tell, whales, antelopes, shrews and giraffes don't sleep at all.

On the other hand, if you are of the hairless primate persuasion, it would be best if you don't try this at home. Going without sleep doesn't work very well for most humans. In fact sleep deprivation is Dirty Trick Number One in every military interrogator's Little Black Book. Dr. Bernard Frankel of the US National Institute of Health says bluntly, "A human being can stay awake for no longer than twelve days without permanent damage."

Besides, it feels good. Sam Coleridge wrote "Oh, sleep! It is a gentle thing, beloved from pole to pole." And it's not as if it's a total waste of time. Fleming dreamed up penicillin while he was asleep. The laws of heredity came to Mendel in his sleep. Einstein discovered the germ of his Law of Relativity during one of his ten-hour timeouts. And Mozart composed *The Magic Flute* with his eyes wide shut.

The way I look at it, sleep is inevitable. So why not lie back and enjoy it?

Pecksniffery

*The British? They don't have sex lives. They
have hot water bottles.*

—Milos Foreman

Ah, it's a hardy stereotype—the frigid Brits. Nightclub co-
medians know they can always score a cheap guffaw by
making fun of passionless limeys and their prissy, stiff-upper-lip-
pish ways.

Anglo-Saxon sang-froid is universally acknowledged, universally disparaged, and as an Englishman himself might say, a
load of utter rubbish.

The British aren't passionless, they just have better manners
(soccer louts excluded) than the rest of us.

As for lacking a sex drive, you've got to be wondering what
bushel basket Milos Forman has been living under for the past
few decades. Did he miss the Profumo Scandal? Fergie, Duchess
of Toes? Prince Charles and Lady Tampon? The veritable daisy
chain of British Members of Parliament who get caught—at a
rate of about once a fortnight—with their Oxfords under the
wrong beds? Near as I can tell, the British are about as randy

a lot as this hormonally overcharged planet has ever spawned. Consider the news from Exeter College at Oxford University, where undergraduates have voted to ban heavy petting.

In the dining room.

They also voted in favour of splitting the junior common room into two areas: one for heavy petting and one for light petting.

Oh, yes, and they also supported a motion banning intercourse in the library between 3:00 a.m. and 8:00 a.m. One has to assume that for the other nineteen hours of the day, boffing in the books enjoys the Exeter College seal of approval.

Doesn't sound like a sex-drive-challenged nation to me.

The Norwegians—there's another group that gets held up to ridicule in the Sexier Than Thou Department. The Norse are cold, the cliché goes. Distant. Aloof. They got no rhythm.

Well, you couldn't prove it by the story that's rocking Norway right now. Norwegian media are busy chronicling the ongoing public quarrel between two women over just exactly whose breasts appeared in a Norwegian magazine recently.

Seems an enterprising photographer snapped a picture of a Norwegian lass strolling along a Canary Island beach with only the bottom part of her bikini performing its function. When the photo appeared in a weekly magazine back home, a distraught woman named Aud Sto sued the publisher for 150,000 kroner, claiming she was the woman who belonged to those breasts, and the publication of the photo had subjected her to ridicule in her rural home town.

Whereupon a second Norse nymph by the name of Inger Marie Maylam surfaced to say that hers, not Ms. Sto's, were the breasts that graced the photo in question. Ms. Maylam also said, "the breasts are mine and they are for free. It is wrong for somebody else to try to make 150,000 kroner on them."

Sounds pretty sexually well-adjusted to me.

Nope, if you want to see sexual uptightness in action, you don't have to leave home. Pecksniffian prudery is alive and well here in the Great White North. Not long ago, some upright citizens in Toronto tried to have a woman arrested for breast-feeding her child in public.

What is the problem here? Why is it I can turn on my TV and see severed heads, full-frontal NHL punch-ups and bullet-riddled bodies on channel after channel, but something as beautiful, unthreatening and utterly healthy as human female breasts instantly tighten the sphincters of Canada's self-appointed censors?

Maybe it's not the breasts at all, maybe it's the idea of breast milk that offends them.

Dunno why. We are talking literally about the staff of life here.

Besides, human breast milk enjoys one advantage that the stuff our dairies sell us will never be able to equal.

Outstanding packaging.

Singing: Bad for Your Health?

Extraordinary how potent cheap music is.
—Noel Coward

Sir Noel was bang on the money with that one. A simple jin-gle can be a cultural powerhouse. A song doesn't have to be well-sung or well-crafted to pack a punch. The lyrics to "Happy Birthday" are inane to the point of fatuity, but we've all sung it dozens of times, and enjoyed every performance. The song "We Will Rock You" could have been written by a tone-deaf twelve-year-old, but fans never tire of roaring that anthem en masse at hockey games and soccer matches.

The power of even a mediocre song can be enormous. It can cheer us up or bum us out. It can inspire or infuriate us; fill us with joy or heartbreak.

Or even kill us.

You think I exaggerate? Tell it to the judge—the judge in Manila in the Philippines, who just got through sentencing an-other Filipino for murder. The defendant had been singing "My Way" in a Karaoke bar, much to the derision of another patron who laughed and jeered at his vocal stylings.

So the crooner pulled out a .38 Smith & Wesson and croaked him.

Hey, "My Way" is a treacly gobbet of sentimental goo even when Sinatra sings it. Nobody should have to hear it sung well, never mind badly. Perhaps it was really a mercy killing.

Bad music hath charms to soothe the most savage of breasts—and beasts. Researchers at the National Sea Life Centre in Birmingham, England, had a problem. Ten sharks—five male, five female—didn't want to play house. Try as they might, they could not induce or entice the finny brutes to heed the call of nature and swim forth and multiply.

Then they discovered Barry White.

Yes, that Barry White, the oleaginous, gold-chain-swaddled tune merchant whose gag-prompting ballads slimed up the music charts back in the sleazy sixties. The researchers discovered that Barry White recordings, played underwater, nudged the sharks into behaviour patterns that looked a lot like piscatorial foreplay.

A spokesperson for the centre said that the previously monk-like sharks "did seem a bit more excited, chasing one another around the tank" after hearing a couple of White CDs.

Well, I dunno. I believe if I was forced to listen to an endless tape loop of Barry White warbling "Can't Get Enough Of Your Love, Babe" and "You're the First, the Last, My Everything," I'd be thrashing around mindlessly and going berserk too. I don't think the sea life centre has an outbreak of shark foreplay on its hands, I think it's a case of Aquarium Rage.

Paula Wolf could relate to that. Paula is a housewife in the town of Poppleton in England.

Correction: Paula used to be a housewife. She is now separated from her husband and seeking divorce. The reason? He refuses to stop imitating Roy Orbison. Four years ago, somebody convinced Dave Wolf that he sounded just like the American singer. Dave liked the idea so much he quit his job and went on the road as an Orbison impersonator.

"It just can't go on," Paula said. "I do like some of the songs, but it all got to be too much. He's more devoted to Roy than to me."

No need to explain, Paula. I'm surprised you didn't drive him up to Birmingham and push him into the shark tank. Bad music—or even mediocre music badly performed—can bring out the worst in anyone. Take my pal Eddie, the guy in the next office. He loves the theme song from *The Titanic*. Matter of fact, he's whistling it right now.

And has been for the past two hours.

Good old Eddie. Sounds like he's having the time of his life.

Which is good, because it's almost over.

A Whole New Way to Lose!

I was speechifying in Regina recently and found myself with a free evening to kill, so I did what I often do in cities when I'm looking for a cheap thrill: I went to a casino.

Not to gamble—hey, I know a mug's game when I see one—just to stroll around and watch.

All casinos are inherently repellent, dedicated as they are to a lethal brew of blood-simple greed and boneheaded gullibility. The idea is to whip the wallet-bearing clientele into a mindless spending frenzy. Thus the cheap drinks, the harsh lights, the never-ending cacophony of pings and boings and bells and sirens.

And the absence of clocks. The folks who run casinos wouldn't want you fretting about a petty thing like time going by.

Yep, casino designers have thought of just about everything to keep the customers in front of the slots or the gaming tables. Ironically enough, that's become a bit of a problem.

Gambling is a sedentary pastime. You don't get much of a cardiovascular workout hoovering loonies into the maw of a one-armed bandit and you don't develop great pecs playing blackjack against the dealer. A dedicated player could get seriously out of shape—even die—before he's lost all his money.

Naturally the casino masterminds are concerned about such

a possibility. Enter Pedal 'N Play and the Money Mill, two casino machines from the drawing boards of an outfit that calls itself the Fitness Gaming Corporation.

These machines are a literal fusion of gambling and recreation technology. Pedal 'N Play is a bicycle welded to a slot machine. The Money Mill is a slot machine combined with a treadmill.

In other words, all those casino addicts steadfastly clutching their plastic buckets of quarters and loonies now have a chance to lose weight as they lose their money.

And just to remind the users of Pedal 'N Play and the Money Mill of what the exercise is really about, the bicycle and the treadmill are programmed to stop functioning whenever their attached slot machines are idle for more than twenty seconds.

A chance to become slim and insolvent at the same time. Does life get any better than that?

The Fitness Gaming Corporation brochure carols that "there is a new generation of health-conscious adults who enjoy gaming, but do not want to be subjected to a smoke-filled casino. Promoting health and fitness on the casino floor will capture a whole new audience of gamblers!"

Well, I suppose. And I suppose marks—fit as a fiddle or fat as Farouk—will continue to stream into casinos with dreams of instant jackpot wealth, even though casinos are the biggest sucker bet this side of moose pasture stock certificates.

That said, I can tell you one surefire way to beat the casino odds: be sure to eat a meal and order a couple of beers while you're there. Food and drinks are usually first-rate in casinos, and cheap as dirt to boot.

Which is natural—they've got other plans for separating you from your money, after all.

Besides, it's the only break you'll ever get from a casino.

The Ravages of Time

I have everything now I had twenty years ago—
except now it's all lower.

—Gypsy Rose Lee

Ah, yes—gravity. Dirty Trick Number Ten in God's *Manual for the Middle-Aged.*

You can pop antioxidant inhibitors like Pez pellets, work out on your Nautilus around the clock and watch *Buns of Steel* videos until your eyes fall out, but sooner or later, gravity Will Have Its Way With You and you will wrinkle, droop and sag. It's the law.

And it's even worse than I thought. There was a charming little news item in the Los Angeles Times recently that indicates gravity saves some of its most ingenious handiwork for the human face.

"Between the ages of 25 and 65," says an article written by Benedict Carey, "the nose stretches by ten percent on average, its tip moving downward by about a quarter of an inch. The brows can shrink by a third of an inch, the ears by slightly more, the cheek tissue by as much as half an inch. Overall, more than thirty percent of a person's facial area may drop from about the mid-face line into fleshy folds below."

Thanks, Benedict. I needed that.

Ah, well. It's not like the ravages of gravity are the only surprises waiting to bushwhack the unwary as they make their way through middle age. Most humans around the age of forty suddenly find they have to hold books and newspapers at arm's length before they can make out the print.

"You have presbyopia," my ophthalmologist informed me cheerfully. "Relax. It's a normal condition of aging. Your eye lenses are losing their elasticity—turning kind of leathery. We in the profession call it 'old eye syndrome.'"

Thanks, doctor. I needed that, too.

My favourite example of the treachery that awaits all of humankind on the threshold of middle age is The Hair Thing. I speak as a hair-impaired person, you understand. At the age of twenty I began to notice that my cute little widow's peak was becoming more of a peninsula. My hairline was receding. Over the next few years I watched, dismally as my peninsula became an island, then an islet, then . . . well, skin, surrounded by a horseshoe-like atoll that ran from ear to ear around the back of my head.

Fine. It was traumatic, but . . . fine. I adjusted to being a bald guy. Came to enjoy it, actually. You meet a better class of person as a bald guy. Besides, I never wanted to be loved for my hair.

But then came Dirty Trick Number Thirteen. Unwanted hair. There comes a day when most aging males discover that they have more hair on their backs than their heads.

Hair on the back. Whose dumb idea was that? And how about hair growing out of your ears? And rogue hairs that suddenly pop out of your eyebrows like hollyhocks on steroids?

Those are just some of the sadistic surprises the aging process springs on all of us. I haven't even mentioned such treats as aching joints, failing hearing, jaded appetites—you know what I mean—and trying to remember where the hell you left the car keys.

Still, I might as well enjoy it, because it looks like I'm going to be here for a while. There are some pretty stout branches on my family tree. Take old Uncle Oscar on my mother's side. He was in to see the doctor for his annual checkup the other day. The doctor couldn't find a thing wrong with him.

"You're in good shape for an old-timer," the doctor told him. "It must run in your family. How old was your father when he died?"

"What makes you think he's dead?" asked Uncle Oscar. "He's ninety and still going strong."

"Impressive. What about your granddad—how long did he live?"

"What makes you think *he's* dead?" says Oscar. "He's a hundred and six—and he's getting married to a twenty-two-year-old next week."

"But that's insane," says the doctor. "Why would he want to marry such a young woman at his age?"

"*Want* to?" says Uncle Oscar, "He *had* to."

Stupid Male Tricks

*My problem is that God gave me a brain and a
penis, but only enough blood to operate one of
them at a time.*

—Robin Williams

Suppose you were a male giant panda. Know what you'd have to do to prove you were the biggest, baddest panda in the whole bamboo patch?

You would have to stand on your hands and pee. As high as you could.

That's right. According to Angela White, a research scientist at the Zoological Society of San Diego, California, male pandas establish their dominance by leaving their urine stains high on nearby rocks or trees. The strongest pandas can actually do handstands to improve their elevation.

Why doesn't this surprise us?

Perhaps it's because handstand peeing contests are not that far removed from a guy in a Diesel tank top and a pair of Ray-Bans playing liver-curdling heavy metal on the stereo of his smoke-windowed Trans-Am with *Big Daddy* stencilled across the windshield.

Stupid macho male tricks. You don't have to be a giant male panda to play them.

You don't have to be human either. Look what male praying mantises put up with to get a little romance. For these critters, going all the way means Going All the Way. Female praying mantises have been routinely chewing up their partners after sex for millions of years. And for all those millennia, male praying mantises have been ignoring the bloodstains on their dates' lips, chanting to themselves the insect equivalent of "Hoo, boy, I'm gonna get lucky tonight."

Either male praying mantises are so stupid they haven't noticed none of their buddies ever make it back to the locker room after sex . . . or worse, they know, but are so horny they don't care.

The male instinct to rut is a powerful one, but not overpoweringly brilliant. The male salmon could end out his days hanging out with his buddies in a nice tidal pool chasing herring and rock cod. But no, he has to hump his way on a suicide mission up waterfalls, over logs, past hungry bears and eagles, all for the thrill of making his deposit on a gravel-bed nest way up some fresh-water creek.

My father, who was a shy man, decided to introduce me to the mysteries of the birds and the bees by taking me at the age of twelve to watch the mating of a mare and a stallion.

Have you ever seen horses mate? It is not hearts and flowers or candlelight and wine. It is not Romeo and Juliet. It's not even Pamela Anderson and Tommy Lee.

It's more like the attack at Dieppe.

There is dust and confusion and squealing and biting. There is much thunder of hooves and whinnying.

And the mare lays a beating on the stallion that makes a guy cross his legs just to think of it. She kicks him. Hard. Where it hurts. A lot of times. The stallion keeps coming back for more.

I shouldn't have been surprised, I guess. After all, as someone once said, our biological drives are several million years older than our intelligence. And a guy in heat is a guy in heat, be he a panda, a praying mantis or a hormone-addled teenager at a Saturday night rave. Probably goes back to Adam and Eve.

As a matter of fact, there's a story about God popping in to the Garden of Eden near the end of the seventh day with just a few odds and ends left in his bag of creations.

One of the things he has left in the bag is the ability to pee standing up. He asks Adam and Eve if either of them would want that ability. Up jumps Adam, yelling, "Oh, give that to me, please! Yes, I'd like to be able to do that. I could really use a talent like that—oh, please, please, please!"

Eve just rolls her eyes. "Since he wants it so badly," she says, "let him have it."

"Fine," says God. "But I must have something for you, too, Eve. Let's see what's left in here. Oh, yes. Multiple orgasms . . . "

The Rule of Thumb

Don't look now, but your body is changing.

On second thought—do look. Look down on those stumpy little appendages that jut out like miniature Floridas from the side of your hands. We call them thumbs. My dictionary defines the thumb as "the first digit on the hand, differing from the other fingers in having only two phalanges (knuckles) and being more flexible and opposable to the other fingers."

Now take your favourite hand and put the tip of your forefinger to the tip of your thumb, making the okay sign.

That, my friend, is what separates you from every other beast on the planet. Some other critters have thumbs, but they're not opposable thumbs. Other animals can't manipulate shovels, knitting needles, screwdrivers, ballpoint pens or the magnification dial on an electron microscope in any meaningful, consistent way—and that's the main difference between Us and Them. Our thumbs gave our ancestors the ability to grasp objects and fashion them into tools: at first crude spears; later farming implements; eventually printing presses, microchip factories and Palm Pilots.

Imagine trying to get through a day without using your thumbs. Imagine trying to make a pot of coffee, do up a zipper, lace up your shoes or even open the door to your car.

Handy little digit, the thumb. Useful in language too. If

we're clumsy, we say that we're all thumbs. We have the option of thumbing our nose at a blind hockey ref or thumbing through a dictionary looking for new things to call him. For years Iraq was under the thumb of Saddam Hussein. We can veto a project by voting thumbs down, or give the go ahead with a thumbs up.

Don't, by the way, give the thumbs-up signal to natives in Sardinia or Greece. It means something quite different there, something North Americans associate with a different upraised digit.

The doughty little thumb has served us well since before the dawn of civilization, and it appears to be morphing into a new phase in order to serve in the ages to come.

Our thumbs are getting bigger.

Dr. Sadie Plant, a researcher at the University of Warwick in England, conducted a survey involving young people under the age of twenty-five in nine cities around the world. Her conclusion? Young people have more powerful thumbs than you and I. In fact their thumbs are already more muscled and dexterous than their other digits.

It's not hard to figure out why. Think Nintendo. Think amusement arcades. Think cellphones.

Back in the old days—which is to say about twenty years ago—much of the world used rotary-dial telephones that were made to be operated by the index finger. But on a hand-held phone with a push-button pad, it's actually easier to punch in a number with your thumb.

Dr. Plant also discovered that young people are increasingly using their thumbs for other chores formerly reserved for the index finger, like ringing doorbells and even pointing.

So it looks like the thumb is coming back, just like the good old, bad old days of Ancient Rome when bloodthirsty crowds in the Coliseum got to use their thumbs to decide the fate of fallen gladiators—right?

Wrong. That's a Hollywood myth. The Romans considered the thumb to be a digital representation of a sword. When they were feeling merciful, they extended their fists with their thumbs tucked in, out of sight. Which is to say, they symbolically sheathed their swords. When they wanted the poor sod killed, they jabbed their thumbs forward in an unequivocal stabbing motion.

Ancient Romans never used the thumbs-up signal.

Unless of course, somebody was tailgating their chariot.

Whine Not!

There's a wonderful old James Thurber cartoon that shows a slightly goofy-looking gent holding a glass of wine by the base (as only winegeeks do) and enthusing, "It's a naïve, domestic burgundy without any breeding, but I think you'll be amused by its presumption."

That's a near-perfect send-up of what I call winebabble: that smarmy, pseudosophisticated bafflegab that you too often hear from the grape-stained lips of wine lovers.

I have no problem with wine descriptions that actually say something. If someone tells me a wine tastes peppery or fruity, that gives me a sense of what they mean. I have no trouble imagining the taste of an oaken port or a woody cabernet. But what the hell is a wine that displays angular resonance? Or virginal overtones? Or a charming presence?

It gets worse. I have heard wines described as "boof." Or "boofless."

Don't ask me.

I read one wine taster's notes on a hapless Rioja. He wrote, "amusing peptides. Hints of the Crimea."

And in a Napa Valley wine store, there's a *chi-chi* little "connoisseur's guide" sitting on a shelf of Sauvignon Blanc that reads, "From the first sniff, one is impressed by the precise, deep but never bombastic aromas in which green apple and crenshaw melon scents mix and by a creamy, vanillin accent of oak, and it is wonderfully balanced on the palate with ripe richness set off by firming acids and brightness."

Talk like that's enough to drive a person to drink.

Wine talk doesn't have to be boring or pretentious. Someone once had the wit to describe a new Zinfandel as a "De Gaulle" wine.

Which is to say, "tall, with an earthy nose, but slightly dead."

The Canadian possibilities are intriguing. We could have a Bertuzzi Burgundy: "surreptitious . . . sneaks up, blindsides you and leaves you for dead."

A Chretien Cabernet: "renders you speechless in both official languages."

A BC Chateauneuf de Liberal: "flat, tasteless, soon to be discontinued."

A Sheila Copps Catawba: "sharp, with a bitter aftertaste."

Oh, but we've already got Newfie Screech.

I think it would be wise if wine tasters developed a sense of humour before the rest of the world dies laughing at their preposterous solemnity.

They might also want to invest in a decent translation service. The following appeared on the label of a shipment of Allozo Crianza, a red wine made in Tomelloso, Spain, and (at last report) sold in select liquor stores across Canada:

"Sensorial tasting. Allozo Crianza has a deep, obscure, red and cherry colour, with a good cloak, clean and brilliant with reflexes of medium evolution that show tiles. It has aromas of breeding, prevailing new wood over an elegant and perfumed bottom of spices, and matured black fruits well united and with balsamic memories. It is vivid on the tongue, with a great acidity very well integrated, a solid, full, silky, and greasy way, and a tasty and well-structured final. It is large and retronasal."

Sounds suspiciously like a wine taster who forgot to spit and rinse.

Don't Just Do Something

Although I'm more Western rustic than Eastern mystic, I'll have you know that I have tried yoga.

I've also tried Pilates, Feldenkraus, 5BX, Dancercize, push-ups and a brisk walk after dinner. That doesn't make me ambitious and athletic. It means that I tend to lose interest in forms of exercise along about the time I start breathing through my mouth and small beads of perspiration appear on my forehead.

Which is why I'm fond of yoga. It's pretty mellow, as exercise regimes go. It's not about building muscle mass or increasing stamina; yoga's about breathing and flexibility. Plus there's no expensive equipment to buy. An old mat and a set of baggy sweats and you're in business.

Well, correction. You're actually out of business. Yoga steers you away from the busy-ness of modern life. Yoga is a system of physical relaxation for sure . . . but it's a mind-rinse too. Which may explain its new-found popularity. Clearly a lot of us feel we're missing out on something in our traffic-jammed, cell-phone-jangled and e-mail-cluttered lives. And just as clearly it's a need that can't be quick-fixed by shrinks, two vodka martinis or forty-five minutes on a stationary bike.

We seem to be looking for a physical workout with a spiritual dimension to it. There's no question that yoga has a spiritual side, but there's also no doubt that it's a workout. For some of us just sitting cross-legged on the ground is a workout.

But that's the great thing about yoga, it's not competitive. You can't earn a black belt in yoga. There are no prizes for Most Contorted Body Position or Longest Meditation. Indeed, if yoga had a bumper sticker, it would read: "Don't just do something; sit there."

Another thing I like about yoga: no minimum fitness requirements. My days as a wide receiver and a rushing defenceman are long behind me, and these creaky knees seize up at the mere thought of a game of racquetball. But I can do yoga until they send the hearse around for me. And what's more, I can do it with my grandparents—and my grandkids. With yoga, age is irrelevant.

Take Mahatma Gandhi. He was a lifelong yoga practitioner who stayed hale and hearty into his eighties. He'd probably still be doing Sun Salutations if an assassin's bullet hadn't cut him down back in 1948.

Gandhi kept his sense of humour lithe and limber too. I can't swear it was the yoga, but something kept that smile on his face and that swing in his gait. Once, late in his life, a reporter asked him, "Mr. Gandhi what do you think of . . . Western Civilization?"

Gandhi's eyes twinkled behind his steel-rimmed glasses and he replied, "I think that would be a good idea."

V

|||

TEC#NOP#OB!A

Body Double Trouble

To the perfectly lovely young woman who approached me in the grocery store this morning: I'm sorry. I apologize. I was neither drunk nor off my medication.

To everyone who wasn't at the grocery store this morning, here's what happened.

I'm standing in the produce section looking for a ripe cantaloupe among the mottled bowling balls before me when suddenly this woman—this total stranger—comes waltzing up the aisle and says, "Hi. Remember me? From the party last week? I'm the one who just moved into Howard's house."

Number one: I don't know any house owner named Howard. In fact I don't even know any indigents named Howard.

Number two: I know perfectly well that I haven't been to any parties recently.

To sum up: I have no idea who this woman is or what she's talking about.

So how do I handle the situation? I do what I always do when someone I've never met engages me in a totally meaningless conversation. I lie.

"Oh, right!" I say. "The party—great party! How could I forget? That's a swell house you've moved into too!"

Why do I behave in this shameful and dishonest fashion? For one thing, the old noodle isn't quite as whipcrack sharp as it used to be. I don't have grey matter upstairs, I have Swiss cheese. I sometimes forget a face. Hell, I sometimes forget entire families. So when I get into a conversation with a (possible) stranger, I pretend I'm with it in order to play for time, on the off chance that I just might remember something.

The other—and more important—reason I feign comprehension is that I have a brother. A brother who is, ahhh, somewhat less mature than I, to be sure. A brother who is obviously not nearly as dashing or charismatic, but a brother who, aside from some totally superfluous cranial fur, looks a lot like Yours Truly.

The fact is, people get us mixed up. A lot. So people often yack away at him under the impression they're conversing with his more elegant brother or vice versa. And since we only live a few kilometres apart, it happens often.

As luck would have it, I ran into my brother downtown just an hour after the grocery store incident.

"Happened again, bro!" I said. "Some wacky woman came up to me in the store, swore she met me at some party. Said I'd remember her because she's living in Howard's place."

He looked at me a little oddly.

"That was Sidney Shannon," he said. "You met her at Molly's birthday party last week. You talked to her for half an hour, spilled your wine on her and ate all the shrimp off her plate."

Oh . . . yeah. Molly's birthday party. It's coming back now.

So anyway, my apologies, Sidney. Just a touch of amnesia brought on by the old war wound. And while I'm in a confessional mood, that guy at the party who tried to make you wear a lampshade and sing "Barnacle Bill the Sailor" with him?

That was my brother.

Tanks But No Tanks

Well, it's been a month now. The uncontrollable tremors in my hands have vanished. I don't seem to be gibbering spontaneously or throwing my arms over my face any more. I haven't had a savage flashback for three nights in a row.

I think perhaps I'm ready to talk about it.

Driving in Italy, I mean. I spent two weeks in the rolling hills of Tuscany, about an hour's drive from Florence.

Well, about an hour's drive in sleepy, conventional Canadian terms, I mean. In terms of Italian driving I was probably about six and a half minutes from Florence.

Although the trip seemed to take several lifetimes.

It's difficult to find words to describe driving in Italy. I'm a bit of a leadfoot myself and I've seen my share of automotive Armageddons. I've been sideswiped in Montreal, rear-ended in Vancouver and tailgated in New York. I've even braved the 401 outside Toronto at the start of a holiday weekend.

But none of that prepared me for Italy.

First of all the roads—as in most of Europe—are much narrower than we Canucks are used to. And twistier, with lots of hairpin turns and sudden junctions.

And then there are the Italian drivers.

I can say quite sincerely that every Italian I met on my holiday was polite, friendly, helpful, generous, kind and thoughtful.

Until he or she got behind the wheel of a car.

The act of driving an automobile transforms the average Italian—signor or signora—into a ravening marauder. A speed freak. A power monger.

Jacques Villeneuve with PMS.

The mission of every Italian driver is to pass your car. Right now. And they will. They will pass you on turns, in towns, on hills, in tunnels, on blind curves. Once I was passed on a two-lane bridge.

By a dump truck.

Italians do not signal when they pass. Nor have they heard of Elmer the Safety Elephant or the old one-car-length-for-every-fifteen-kilometres-per-hour adage. They believe in zero car lengths between vehicles. At any speed.

As for tailgating, you couldn't call what Italian drivers do just before they pass you tailgating. Italian cars attempt copulation with your car.

The official speed limit on the Autostrada—Italy's super-highway system—is 130 kilometres per hour, but if you ever tried to observe that limit you would die very quickly. Most vehicles routinely maintain at least twice that speed. The rest go even faster.

It's no better off the Autostrada. Oh, the drivers ratchet it back a bit—just enough so their cars don't fly right off the road—but they still hare along at speeds guaranteed to give a North American driver a heart attack.

The only thing worse than being on an Italian road in a car is being on an Italian road without a car. You get the impression that for most Italian drivers pedestrians are simply an exotic form of potential roadkill. My guide book actually offered this road crossing advice: "Walk out slowly and confidently," it says, "glaring at the traffic and maintaining a determined pace. The traffic should stop. Or at least swerve."

Yeah, right. And if that works, you might want to try walking on water.

Would I ever go back to Italy? Listen. Italy is easily one of

the most beautiful places I have ever visited and the people—
once you divest them of car keys—are a total delight. The food is
wonderful, the scenery is spectacular, the art treasures are priceless and the wine is just grand.

So would I go back to Italy? In a heartbeat . . . and a Sherman
tank.

The Incredible Disappearing Cellphone

Got on the bus the other day and sat down across from a guy who was cleaning his ear. Gross, I thought. Then I realized he was also talking to himself, or rather, to his wrist. Which is when I clued in; I'm a slow learner. The guy was simply using his cellphone.

In a public place, in a loud, obnoxious voice, telling the rest of the passengers way more than any of us wanted to know about his abysmally boring day job—but that's another rant.

No, the point I want to make here is that his cellphone was so small there was a danger of it getting lodged in his ear. Why are cellphones getting so damned tiny?

Years ago—and not that many, come to think of it—cellphones were the size of bread loaves. They were huge, ungainly things you could use for a doorstop. Granted they were ugly and cumbersome, but I think we've gone too far in the other direction. Cellphones today are so diminutive they fold down to about the size of a business card.

Which would be fine except for one drawback: physiology. God is still turning out human models with the same size of hands. Those hands include fingers that were never designed to hunt and peck through a cellphone number pad that's not much bigger than a postage stamp. I note that one cellphone manufacturer is now offering a pointy little stylus that fits over the end of your dialling finger, allowing you to punch one button at a time instead of three.

We doan need no steenkin' stylus . . . what we need is a human hand-sized number pad.

And it's not just cellphones. The same thing applies to PDAs, handheld electronic games and hotel radios. Ever tried to change the station or set the alarm on the bedside radio in your hotel room? Who are those things designed for, leprechauns?

The communications business is going nuts over miniaturization right now, and it's getting dangerous. If you don't believe me, ask Antonio Mendoza of Los Angeles. Mr. Mendoza, an attorney at law, has just been released from his local medical trauma centre, following the successful removal of his cellphone from his, er, rectum.

"My dog drags the thing all over the house," he explained. "He must have dragged it into the shower. I slipped on the tile and sat right down on the thing."

Bad enough, right? How would you like to explain to the admissions nurse why you needed to see a doctor pretty quick? But the story gets worse. It took doctors more than three hours to perform the extraction, because the cover to Mr. Mendoza's phone had opened during insertion.

That's right. Throughout the operation, Mr. Mendoza was . . . getting calls.

"He was a real trouper during the entire episode," said one doctor. "Three times during the extraction the phone rang, and each time, he made jokes about it."

Mr. Mendoza is back at work now, walking a little gingerly, but otherwise none the worse for wear. Obviously, he's a resourceful, outgoing, fun-loving guy—if a tiny bit clumsy.

Just don't ask him to turn the other cheek.

Delete This

Had coffee the other day with a friend of mine. An ex-cop. He'd been on the force for eight or ten years, then suddenly last spring he'd resigned.

And now it seemed like he might want to talk about it.

I wasn't sure just how to approach the subject. There was a rumour going around that my friend had suffered a nervous breakdown. But why? Did the constant stress of facing down crazed crackheads and homicidal psychopaths finally get to him? Was it the unrelenting threat of injury and death? The strain of dealing with the human race at its violent, booze- and dope-fuelled worst? Was that what got to him? I asked as gently as I could.

His hand shook slightly as he hoisted the mug to his lips.

"No," he said softly. "It was the paperwork."

My friend estimated that he spent three-quarters of each working day making notes, sending memos, filling in forms and typing out reports.

"I wasn't a policeman," he said, "I was an office clerk who happened to carry a gun."

It wasn't the pressure of holding down one of the world's most dangerous jobs that got to him. It was the mind-numbing boredom of shuffling paper all day long.

My pal is not alone. A business consultant by the name of

Dianna Booher recently conducted a survey of two thousand businesses. A few of her conclusions:

White-collar office workers spend sixty percent of their time checking, filing and retrieving printed information.

Of all the documents that are printed, copied and distributed by North American businesses every day, seventy-five to eighty percent are never referred to again.

For every dollar spent thinking up documents, it costs up to eighty dollars to print, copy, distribute, file and eventually destroy them.

But that's old news, because this is the age of the computer, right? Paper shuffling is obsolete in the Brave New Electronic World of the Internet and e-mail.

Wrong. A study from San José State University concludes that computers have not replaced old technology, they've merely jumped on its back, adding to the burden.

Office workers don't answer just the regular mail any more. They also have to respond to interoffice mail, voice mail, teleconferencing, e-mail, faxes, pagers—even Post-it Notes. Remember how e-mail was supposed to revolutionize our postal habits by weaning us of our paper habit? Maybe it would if we trusted it, but we don't. Sixty percent of all e-mail is still copied onto paper.

The supreme irony of all those great new space-age time-saving communication devices is that using them consumes more, not less, of our time. Seventy percent of the people interviewed by the San José researchers complain that they are overwhelmed in their personal and professional lives just sending and receiving messages.

Some of us are fighting back. A few office workers ease their burden by deliberately allowing the batteries on their pagers and cellphones to run down. Other people just leave the dust cover on their home computer monitors. I heard of one CEO in California who returned to his desk after vacation to find more than two thousand e-mail messages waiting for him.

His solution? The delete button. He vaporized the whole works.

"I figure if they were really important messages, the senders would get back to me," he explained.

And my friend, the ex-cop?

Sold his computer. Turned in his cellphone. Applied for an unlisted telephone number and landed a job in the hardware department of the local Canadian Tire. Goes fishing on his days off.

And he smiles. A lot.

Way more than he did as a cop.

Smile, You're on Candid Camera!

Had a touch of excitement on my leisurely tootle into town this morning. Came over a hill and spotted a woman in a van parked at the side of the road. She had the driver's window down and she was pointing a gun right at me.

What did I do? Took my foot off the gas pedal, of course. The woman in the van was a Mountie and the roscoe in her mitt was a radar gun.

It's always a bit of a jolt when somebody points a gun your way. When it's a radar gun you have a situation that is both alarming and potentially expensive.

Mind you, we've got it soft. Canadian cops are pussycats in the speed trap department. If you want to be well and truly bushwhacked and shaken down by the boys in blue, head south, my friend.

To US highway 301 in north central Florida, to be precise. It runs through two little whistle-stop burgs named Lawtey and Waldo. Eleven hundred people call Waldo home and about seven hundred live in Lawtey. They're fishing villages, really—except the catch isn't fish—it's cars. Each year the two towns rake in over a half a million US dollars in "highway revenue."

How do they do it? Piracy, pure and simple. The local constabulary sees to it that ridiculously low speed limit signs are posted around blind curves and in dips in the road. Then they park their unmarked cruisers on the shoulder a few hundred metres further down the road and wait for the fish to arrive. Pretty soon they're flagging down "speeders" as fast as they can wave.

The fines they levy are outrageously high and the amounts are whatever the cop feels like making up, because they often don't even bother with radar.

Mind you, the drivers don't have to pay right away, they can always go directly to jail. There's a knee-jerk justice of the peace who's always on call and more than willing to rubber stamp them right into the local slammer, which will never be mistaken for the Ritz Carlton. The drivers—mostly tourists and frequently Canadian—usually cough up on the spot.

A spokesperson for the American Automobile Association admits it's an unbelievable situation. "It's amazing these towns are allowed to exist in this day and age. The fines represent seventy-five percent of Lawtey's total revenue and fifty percent of Waldo's. These two towns are writing more tickets than Miami."

Actually, there's a whole stretch of highway that extends up through Georgia and West Virginia where motorists run a speed-trap gauntlet. They ought to rename it the Spanish Main.

But even legitimate speed traps—if that's not an oxymoron—are infuriating, because basically we're getting fined for being dumb. We know we shouldn't speed, but there we are, fumbling through our wallet to find our driver's licence and registration while we stammer out half-baked excuses to a clearly unamused officer of the law.

Still, it is nice to know that once in awhile the jackboot is on the other foot.

As in the case of two constables in the Lothian district of Scotland who were nailing motorists left and right with a radar gun recently, when suddenly the speed gauge on the gun went bananas, recording an approaching vehicle travelling in excess of five hundred kilometres an hour.

It was about that point that the RAF Harrier jet screamed over the cops at treetop level and disappeared.

The radar gun was fried and the cops were ticked—even made an official complaint to the local Air Force base.

Which is when they found out the experience could have been a lot uglier. An RAF spokesperson explained that the Harrier's target-seeker had locked on to what it had interpreted as enemy radar. This should have triggered an automatic air-to-surface missile attack on the police cruiser and its hapless occupants. Lucky for them the Harrier wasn't carrying missiles that day.

I'm glad that aside from a traumatized radar gun no harm was done.

But I still want to buy that pilot a beer.

Coffee, Tea or Me?

This may just be the jet lag talking—I've been hopscotching by air all over the continent for the past several days—but . . .

What is it about airports?

A person ought to feel great in an airport. After all, it's a slick, no-hassles city in miniature. You've got your restaurants, your bookstores, your newspaper kiosks, even your chapels and your lost and founds. At the really big airports you can get a shoeshine, a bottle of Dom Perignon and a massage.

Airports are totally climate-controlled. Once you get inside those doors you don't have to deal with heat waves, monsoons or black ice. You also don't have to worry about being run over by a truck, getting stuck in a traffic jam or being mugged by a gang of Homies.

And the airport is ecumenical. Hardline Muslims line up at the check-in counter, cheek by jowl with staunch Catholics; fundamentalist Baptists share leatherette couches with Unitarians; dreadlocked Wiccans break bread with briefcase-toting burghers from the 'burbs.

Your average big city airport is nothing if not democratic. We should love them. Vast armies of the homeless and the dispossessed ought to be pressing up against the hurricane fencing around our airports, eager to get inside and set up camp. Names like O'Hare and Heathrow, Pearson and Nagoya ought to be mentioned in the same breath as London and Bangkok, Vienna and Paris.

So how come that doesn't happen? Why is it airports make us nervous, antsy and eager to be just about anyplace else?

Perhaps it's the very nowhereness of modern airports. Being in Gatwick is like being in Kennedy is like being in Dallas International. The same disembodied mechanical voices reverberating off the same marble surfaces.

And it's a false community. Sure, you're surrounded by every hue and accent of the human race, but like you, they're all going somewhere else—and soon! These people you've been thrown together with you'll probably never see again. The airport "community" has the shelf life of a champagne bubble. Maybe something in our genetic makeup recognizes that and keeps us on standby alert.

One saving grace is that most of us don't have to deal with airports all that often. Pity the poor folks—the maintenance people, the caterers, the guys who have to hump our luggage around—everyone who has to work in airports, day in and day out.

Mind you, they occasionally have their revenge. Like the Canadian Airlines gate agent who had to process an entire daisy chain of disgruntled travellers when a flight out of Ottawa was cancelled. She was working her way through the line with as much grace as she could muster when a red-faced guy in a three-piece suit bulled his way to the front of the line. He slapped his ticket down on the counter and said, "I *have* to be on this flight and it has to be *first class*."

The agent replied, "I'm sorry, sir. I'll be happy to try to help you, but I've got to help these folks first, and I'm sure we'll be able to work something out." The passenger was unimpressed. He asked loudly, so that the passengers behind him could hear, "Do you have any idea who I am?"

Without hesitating, the gate agent smiled and grabbed her public address microphone.

"May I have your attention, please?" she began, her voice bellowing throughout the terminal. "We have a passenger here at the gate *who does not know who he is*. If anyone can help him find his identity, please come to Gate 17."

With the folks behind him in line laughing hysterically, the man glared at the Canadian Airlines agent, gritted his teeth and hissed, "Screw you!"

Flashing her best flight attendant smile, the agent purred, "I'm sorry, sir, but I'm afraid you'll have to stand in line for that too."

Does Colour Matter?
Of Cars It Does!

You can have any colour you want. As long as it is black.

—Henry Ford

Y ou always know when the Canadian poet Susan Musgrave is coming down the road. The car she drives is neither new nor sporty—pretty conventional, in fact.

Aside from the fact that it is completely covered—and I mean doors, hood, trunk, fenders and bumpers—with glued-on kids' toys.

There's an art teacher in Nanaimo, BC, who encourages his students to treat his pickup as a canvas. He lets them paint anything they want on it, and then he grades their creations.

There's a guy in Florida who drives an '85 Chevy that's covered with green, growing grass. There's a guy in New York who drives a car covered with clocks. And there's an artist in Santa Cruz, California, who maintains a stable of two Volkswagen beetles that he's converted to look like flying saucers.

The question is not what drug these folks are on. The question is: what's wrong with the rest of us? Why this slavish indulgence to the measly four or five colours the big automakers parcel out each fall? You don't have to be Sigmund Freud to figure out that your car is in some way an extension of yourself. So how come we don't spontaneously personalize our cars the way we decorate our living rooms, front porches and backyards?

The interesting thing is that car buyers' tastes do change, if only within the parsimonious parameters meted out by the car manufacturers. From 1994 to 1998 the most popular new car colour in North America was green. In 1999 people purchased more white cars than any other colour. In the year 2000, nineteen percent of all North American new-car buyers chose silver.

Not surprisingly, our car-buying habits and the colours we choose are a psychological gold mine for shrinks. A recent study commissioned by the British Broadcasting Company concluded that we choose our car colours as a clear signal to other motorists. A white car, the experts say, indicates a distant, aloof demeanour, while Type A personalities gravitate toward black.

You want to be a magnet for road-ragers? Get yourself a fire-engine-red buggy. There's something about red that brings out the psychotic in fellow travellers. Mind you, you'll also be a prime target for any cop with a radar gun. The shrinks say that people who drive red cars like to put the pedal to the metal.

Traffic control officers say, "we've noticed."

Then there's the neutral family of car colours—champagne, gold and lighter shades of brown. They make up about fifteen percent of all vehicles purchased last year and the year before that.

The colour of my car? I was afraid you'd ask. It's a bland and boring variation of beige, and yes, I actually chose it. Not because I liked the shade, but because I liked the other options less. I like to delude myself that one of these days I'll buy a half-dozen cans of Day-Glo spray paint and customize the crate.

Of course, it would help to be rich. Like the friend of Phil Silvers, the TV comedian. It bugged this rich guy that he could never figure out an original gift to give Silvers; the guy had everything already.

One Friday, Silvers arrived at his friend's villa to spend the weekend. As Silvers drove up—in a Rolls Royce Silver Cloud—inspiration struck.

"Sounds like it's idling a little rough," the friend said to Silvers. "You're not going to need it all weekend. Let me have my mechanic tune it up for you."

The host then had the car (unbeknownst to Silvers) whisked off to a deluxe auto repair shop, where a specially hired crew worked around the clock to tear out the interior of the car and replace it with a customized bar, a colour television set and a state-of-the-art stereo system. The Rolls was delivered back to the estate just before Silvers was to leave Monday morning. Escorting him to the car, the host murmured, "Before you start out, Phil, maybe you should check everything out to make sure it's in shape."

"Oh, that doesn't matter," said Silvers. "It's only a rental."

Some Assembly Required

One of my favourite stories about Steven Spielberg—actually, my only story about him—is one that his wife tells. One night in his Hollywood home, the guru of technological space movie wizardry complained about the heat.

"Turn the thermostat down," his wife said.

"What's a thermostat?" asked Spielberg.

His wife pointed out the plastic doohickey on the bedroom wall. Spielberg looked at it like it was an artifact from the asteroid Archilochos.

"No kidding," he said. "How does it work?"

My kind of man.

I, too, am a technophobe. The last mechanical device I had any hope of actually understanding was my one-speed CCM bike, circa 1956. Mountain bikes mystify me. Hell, oven toasters mystify me. I have a TV set with access to three hundred channels—so I'm told. I have to get Ruby to turn it on for me.

Ruby is my niece. Aged fourteen.

My computer? You don't want to know about my computer. I have mastered turning it on and turning it off and even typing a few pages (screens?) and printing them off. But that's only because I have painstakingly hand-lettered step-by-step Post-it Notes that are pasted across the bottom of my monitor, marching me through the process. And it never goes smoothly.

That's why my fourteen-year-old niece is required to observe a hundred-metre Profanity No-Go Zone when Uncle Art is duelling *mano a mano* with his computer.

But it doesn't require the presence of working electrons to leave me in the dust. I never, for instance, program VCRs. When desperate maidens flag me down on the highway begging for a boost, I wave and shrug and smile haplessly, pretending I have no battery cables.

I have battery cables. They are still in the original cellophane. Because I can't remember if the #&^%@+* things go positive to negative or positive to positive.

Not to mention which is black and which is red.

I am a technophobe. Which is a sorry thing to be in this mercilessly technocratic age in which we live.

Even sorrier when you consider that I don't live within the same telephone exchange as Ted Stewart.

Ted is the answer to a technophobe's dreams. He lives in Fredericksburg, Virginia, and each working day he hops into his truck—the one full of screwdrivers and hammers and gauges and saws and awls and levels and miter boxes and all the other sundry mysteries of the handyman's trade, and . . .

. . . saves the bacon of technophobes like me.

Ted is a freelance Mr. Fixit. He can put up to five hundred kilometres a day on his pickup, roaming the suburbs of Virginia to bail out all-thumbs nerdballs like me who can't put together their back decks or pool tables or hot tubs or exercise gyms.

Ted is intimately familiar with no-talent bozos like myself. "These guys just don't want to mess with stuff, or they don't know how," says Ted. "There are a lot of guys who don't know how to turn a wrench."

Oh, well said, Ted. I don't want to alarm you, but there are certain guys out there who aren't exactly sure what *constitutes* a wrench. Those flat steel things that look like Mr. Magoo's mouth on each end, right? I knew that.

Anyway, Ted runs a one-man company called Some Assembly Required, which bails out klutzes like me and is just about the best business idea I've heard since Adam 'n Eve Apple Products Inc.

Mind you, he has rules.

"If I come in and do the job, it's one price. If you want to help, it's another price. And if you've already attempted to build it on your own, it's going to cost even more."

Sure, Ted, I can live with that. And I could use your help. Real soon, actually. I'm going to call you up and make an appointment.

Just as soon as I can find somebody to help me turn on this @*&%$!^ cellphone.

Back to the Future

*In the early days of radio, people regarded
wireless talking as a mysterious form of
communication. Some listeners thought it
necessary to leave windows open to receive radio
waves. The BBC's first program in 1922 was
followed by a slow repetition of the information,
so that listeners could take notes if they wished.*
        —News item, *Globe and Mail*

As a guy who spent thirty years working in radio, you might
think I'd know just about everything there is to know
about the medium. Not so. Some of the simplest things about
radio baffle me.

Why, for instance, when I'm listening to an interview, do I
hear the host say, "Please make your answer brief because we're
running out of time." Why is he running out of time? Because
it's 7:28 a.m. and the news comes on at 7:30. My question: who
cares?

Would you mind if the news started at 7:32 a.m. instead of
bang on the half-hour? Wouldn't make any difference to me.

The reason for radio's near-fanatical devotion to the clock is that radio is scripted right down to the second. Every newscast, every interview, every commentary and commercial you hear is or has been read off a sheet of paper or a computer screen. And why is that? Why couldn't radio be more natural? It's just people talking, after all.

Garrison Keillor has a theory about that. Keillor, aside from being a master of talking on the radio, is author of a book called *WLT: A Radio Romance.* In the book Keillor speculates that the problem with radio is that it was invented in the wrong order.

"It belonged to the age of bards and storytellers who squatted by the fire, when all news and knowledge was transmitted by telling." Keillor figures that the written word, by coming first, hobbled radio. "Literature had taken radio and hung scripts around its neck, choking the free flow of expression that alone could give radio life. Scripts made radio cautious, formal, tight, devoted to lines. But radio is not lines—radio is air!"

Maybe Keillor is onto something; maybe he's just blowing hot air, but wouldn't it be interesting if some innovations that we take for granted had been discovered in a different order? If, say, the electric typewriter had been invented *after* the computer printer? "Marge, look at this! As soon as you hit a key you get your hard copy! You don't have to wait for the printer to spit it out!"

Or what if contact lenses had preceded eyeglasses instead of the other way around? Can't you hear the spectacle ads? "All new, totally portable eyeglasses! Put 'em on or take 'em off whenever you like! Say goodbye to sticking annoying, painful chunks of plastic in your eyes!"

What if cable TV had come before the old twelve-channel, rabbit-eared model? Imagine having the convenience of only twelve channels to monitor instead of 578. Imagine not having to wade through a TV guide the size of the Hong Kong phone book just to find out if *Law & Order* is on tonight.

Or how about telephones? Imagine if cellular phones had been invented before pay phones.

What a breakthrough. No more humping a lump of plastic around on your hip or in your purse all day. No more annoying interruptions in the middle of conversations or while you're riding the bus. No monthly charges. No more annoyingly cutesy-poo ads featuring Jamie Lee Curtis or Candace Bergen.

All replaced by a series of handy, tasteful public telephone kiosks, where for a mere two bits you can call anyone in your listening area—or you can call Pop in Pensacola and reverse the charges. Most important: you can call out; nobody else can call in.

Edgar Degas, the French painter and sculptor, had a nasty feeling about the telephone right from the get-go. Once he was invited to dinner by a friend who had just had one of the new-fangled contraptions installed in his home. In order to impress Degas, this friend had arranged to have someone telephone during dinner. The phone rang, the friend jumped up to answer it and returned to the table, beaming with pride.

"So that is the telephone," Degas mused sourly. "It rings and you run."

Drop That Elephant Right Now

I was sitting near the rear of a cross-town bus pretending to read my paper but actually, covertly, spying on these three young teenaged kids across the aisle. They were all boys, all dressed in the regulation watch cap, hooded sweatshirt and baggy pants that seem to be *de rigueur* for all young teenaged rugged individualists these days. The boys were scrunched over in their seats, like medieval supplicants, heads down, frantically manipulating plastic lozenges in their laps, lozenges that beeped and blipped incessantly.

Nintendo addicts.

They didn't know I was alive, and that's okay. I doubt that any teenagers in history have ever been aware they shared the planet with other, older or younger people. That's the nature of teenagerdom.

But it made me sad all the same, because looking at these kids, these electronic surfers, I was pretty sure that none of them had ever known the pleasure of owing a good, old-fashioned slingshot.

I can't imagine being a young boy and not having—or at least coveting—a slingshot. It was what boyhood was all about . . . going down by the creek and searching among the saplings until you found that elusive tree crotch that formed a perfect Y. Cutting it down, peeling back the bark, whittling perfect notches to hold the rubber band.

Slingshots were forbidden, of course. Parents warned us never to fool with them. Policemen confiscated them on sight. Teachers would send you to the principal if they saw one jutting out of your back pocket.

So naturally we adored them.

I was totally infatuated with my slingshot. Right up until I knocked the window out of Old Man Winthrop's garage with it. It wouldn't have been so bad if Old Man Winthrop hadn't been working in the garage at the time, looked up at the sound of tinkling glass and seen me standing there with eyes as big as golf balls, incriminating slingshot in my hand, the rubber band still swinging in the breeze.

Later that night, my father convinced me that my future would be infinitely brighter if I eschewed playing with slingshots thenceforth.

Not so Hew Kennedy. Kennedy lives on a farm in Shropshire, England, and although he's approaching middle age, he's never lost his love of slingshots.

Which explains the trebuchet in his backyard.

Trebuchet? That would be the granddaddy of all slingshots. A huge, hulking behemoth of a catapult that looks like a kind of giant, twenty-metre-long spoon attached to a five-tonne weight. Hew Kennedy's trebuchet can throw very heavy objects up to 140m at speeds of up to 140kph.

How heavy? Oh, heavy like a sofa, a grand piano or a dead pig.

"A good, big sow is really aerodynamic," says Kennedy. And he should know. He's hurled all of those and more on his trebuchet.

He's not the first, not by several centuries. Back in Roman times, legionaries employed trebuchets to lay siege to castles. They would lob huge boulders, burning bundles of hay—even dead horses—over the castle walls to wreak havoc among the inhabitants.

But Hew Kennedy isn't laying siege to any castles. He just likes slinging things around the countryside. "It's bloody good fun," says Kennedy.

It's also lucrative. Hew Kennedy and his trebuchet have become a bit of a tourist attraction in Shropshire. Film crews from Japan, Germany and the Scandinavian countries keep knocking on Kennedy's door, asking if he'll activate the trebuchet while their cameras record the event for posterity.

He also gets requests from the odd rich American family which is happy to pay just so "the kids get to see it fling something." Kennedy's happy to oblige—if the price is right.

It's not a bad living, but when I talked to Kennedy he indicated that he's getting a little bored with the repetitive nature of his hobby. Possibly because he's just bought an elephant.

Actually, it's a mechanical elephant, powered by a Ford engine, covered with what looks like elephant skin and featuring four pylon-sized legs that clomp along just like a real elephant.

Jumbo, Kennedy's robot elephant, can carry up to four kids at a time on its back. It's quite popular as well . . . but truth to tell, Kennedy is beginning to tire of Jumbo too. He's looking for new thrill horizons to conquer.

Now if he could just figure out a way to lever Jumbo into the trebuchet . . .

Forget Osama,
Watch Out for Your Pants!

It is a hazardous and unpredictable orb of rocks and gases that you and I inhabit, old chum. Never mind the omnipresent threat of rogue meteorites, runaway floral delivery vans, or raving nutters toting homemade thermonuclear devices in Kids "R" Us satchels on the cross-town bus—never mind all that.

Have you considered the threat of . . .

Tea cozies?

Toilet roll holders?

False teeth?

I thought not.

According to this report from the UK's Department of Trade and Industry which I'm holding before me in asbestos mitts, there's been an eighty-five percent increase in hospital admission injuries over the past three years from human encounters with . . . tea cozies.

Tea cozies, for those of you too callow and untried to have experienced the entire spectrum of tannic beverages, are little woollen thingies that one puts around teapots to keep the tea warm. Folks have been doing it for eons. Think of them as Iron Age thermal blankets.

Tea lovers have been unaccountably tripping, slipping and

otherwise maiming themselves on tea cozies more often in the past few years. And that's not the half of it.

Toilet roll holders have laid 329 innocent bystanders (okay, by-sitters) low since 1999. Treacherous encounters with false teeth incapacitated a further 933 souls. And a mind-boggling 16,662 British citizens required medical assistance after going toe to toe with . . . sofas. Or davenports. Or chesterfields. Instruments of the devil by any name.

But tea cozies, toilet rolls, sofas, all of these societal snakes-in-the-grass pale before truly the most treacherous and unpredictable enemy of modern humankind.

I am referring, of course, to men's trousers.

According to this British Department of Trade and Industry report, there were an astounding—I can barely type this—5,945 personal injuries attributed to "trouser incidents" in one year alone. Why, even chainsaws accounted for a mere 1,207 injuries!

What kind of "trouser incidents"? I quote verbatim:

"Patient had just filled his car with petrol, spilt some on his trousers, went to a friend's house, lit a cigarette and his trousers caught fire."

"Rushing downstairs to rescue the shepherd's pie cooking in the kitchen, caught foot in wide leg of trousers, fell whole flight to hall floor, landed on wrist."

"Playing on pavement outside house, trying to be Sporty Spice, doing a high kick, fell onto kneecap on road surface."

"Patient ironed trousers whilst still wearing them."

"Gluing son's toy together with ultra-bond superglue. Tube of glue burst, patient glued ring onto finger and trousers to leg."

Oh, there is no end of deviltry that a pair of trousers will wreak on an unsuspecting male. I once knew a forest ranger, one of whose sad duties it was to haul drowned anglers out of lakes and rivers each year.

"Know what they almost always have in common?" he asked

me over a beer. "Open flies. Most of them were trying to pee out of their boat, lost their balance, fell in and drowned."

A cautionary tale. I've carried a tin bucket in my boat ever since.

Reminds me of the most accident-prone would-be burglar I've ever heard of.

Back in 1978, a chap by the name of Christopher Fleming decided to break into a Chinese restaurant in Devon, England. He broke a kitchen window, crawled in and was making for the cash register when he lost his balance and fell into the chip fryer. The chip fryer was full of grease; the night was cold.

As the grease congealed, and the burglar alarm pealed, Christopher filled his pockets with change from the cash register and attempted to sprint to safety. Alas, the grease was getting really hard. His sprint turned into a canter, then a trot, then a slow-motion streeeeeeetch.

When the coppers put the cuffs on him, he was all but statuesque.

One can only hope his fly was up.

Gimme Shelter

They say that to tell a story properly, you should fix it in terms of place and time.

Okay. I live on a small Canadian island that is unsophisticated enough to have no stop lights, no four-lane highways, no mega-malls and no bridges connecting it to The Rest Of Canada.

It does, however, fall under the yawning umbrella of Canadian jurisprudence. And that fact has local lawyers (alas, we have them too) scritching their talons in glee.

It's all about a bus shelter, you see. A bus shelter for schoolkids.

What happened was a couple of parents with school-aged children got tired of seeing their kids shivering in the rain and gloom each morning while they waited for the school bus. So they built a bus shelter for them.

The shelter is neat and trim, well back from the road. It keeps the kids out of the wind and rain. But it is cursed with one fatal flaw.

The builders neglected to get a permit.

That means that, should kids huddled in the structure fall victim to an asteroid strike or a rogue logging truck commandeered by Taliban loonies, then there would be what lawyers lovingly refer to as "a liability issue."

In other words, lawsuits would start flying like autumn leaves, and who's gonna pick up the tab?

Not the schoolboard, not the provincial government and not what passes for local government either. They've all refused to take responsibility. Unless there's a virulent outbreak of rational thinking, it looks like the shelter—and others like it—will be torn down.

It's not as if we haven't seen this before. On the outskirts of the Ontario town where I used to live, there's an old stone quarry full of water. Well, not full. The water's about ten metres down from the rim of the quarry, but it's deep and warm in the summer months. It's been a favourite swimming hole for folks in the area for generations.

Until one night a few years back when a guy, after methodically working his way through a twenty-sixer of rum, staggered to the edge and threw himself off.

He broke his back. And then he did what so many moral midgets are doing these days. He sued.

And won a settlement of $1.3 million.

The government then spent another small fortune erecting a steel and concrete fence around the perimeter of the quarry, setting up an attendant's booth and hiring staff to patrol the quarry during daylight hours.

You can still swim in the quarry, but it's somewhat less than a wilderness experience, and all because some witless boozehound was too stunned to keep himself out of harm's way.

I read recently that a smoker in California who is in the process of dying from lung cancer had his court damages award reduced to a mere one hundred million dollars. A judge who reviewed the case felt that the original award of three billion dollars granted by a jury was excessive.

Ten cents would be excessive. This moron had sucked up two packs of Marlboros every day for forty years. He claimed to be unaware that there was any health hazard.

You know what we need? I can't believe I'm writing this, but we need a new government body—some agency that will wade through hordes of frivolous lawsuits and the pettifogging bureaucratic rats' nests of over-regulation that snarl up our lives. We could call it The Ministry of Stupid Litigation. It would be charged with weeding out the greed-driven lawsuits initiated by folks who are merely trolling the courts in search of an undeserved jackpot.

It's a pretty simple concept: actions have consequences. If you smoke, you increase your chances of dying ugly. If you drink and dive into a quarry, you may get hurt. Whatever happens, it's your fault, not the taxpayers'.

As for the illegal structure sitting on the side of a road on my island: it's a shelter for schoolchildren, for God's sake.

Find something significant to get neurotic about.

Computers and Poetry? Why Not?

There's a guy in my town named Herc. He is shortish but extremely muscular. Think human fire hydrant. The word on Herc is: don't mess with him. Oh, he's friendly and gregarious enough, most times. But he's also as tough as a platoon of Ninjas, and if you incur his wrath, your allotted span on this planet can be measured in nanoseconds.

Which is why it was unusual to see Herc lined up at the local Libation Emporium one day, grinning like a man who'd won the Lotto 6/49.

"You're looking mighty chipper today, Herc," said the checkout clerk. "What's up?"

Herc smiled a smile as wide as the federal deficit and said, "Just walked down to the end of the bleepin' dock"—Herc swears a mite—"with my bleepin' computer, an' I hove that bleeper as far as I could inta the harbour.

"And it felt so bleepin' good that I went back home, got my printer and I hove that motherbleeper in after it!"

I know exactly how Herc feels. I love my computer when it's doing what I want it to do. Which would be about one-point-three percent of the time.

The rest of the time I hate my computer. I hate it more than Eaton's hated Simpson's. More than Alberta hated Trudeau. More than Tyson hated Holyfield.

If I could find an ear on my computer I would gnaw it off.

But I can't. I can't find much of anything on my computer. That's the point.

I could probably live with my handicap if only my computer wasn't so bleeping smug. I'll be working away on it when suddenly my monitor screen will go into a kind of graphic stomach cramp and a message will flare across the screen: "This program has performed an illegal function and will be shut down."

What? What illegal function? I paid for this computer! I'm over twenty-one!

Another favourite computer moment occurs when I painstakingly type in some incredibly stupid Internet address—(http://LiZard~xanadu/medusa/@#&phrymzik.com)—the computer clicks and whirrs, and this message pops up on my screen: "Could not connect to [1.135.245.49].

Cause: connection timed out. (10060)"

Gee, thanks, Bill Gates. I can sure work with clear and concise info like that.

No point in appealing to your friendly neighbourhood computer geeks. They understand this gobbledygook! It makes sense to them! Nope, folks, we're on our own.

Well . . . maybe not quite.

I hear that the honchos at Sony Vaio Programming in Tokyo have replaced the stupid and meaningless Microsoft error messages with . . . haiku poetry. Which my dictionary defines as: a very short Japanese style of poetry, consisting of three lines.

And how does that apply to computer error messages? Try these:

> *A file that big?*
> *It might be very useful*
> *But now it is gone.*

> *First snow, then silence.*
> *This thousand dollar screen*
> *Dies so beautifully.*

A crash reduces
Your expensive computer
To a simple stone.

And my personal favourite:

Windows NT crashed.
I am the blue screen of death.
No one hears your screams.

Computer programming with a sense of literature *and* a sense of humour? What next? Macintosh?

See You Later, Elevator

Is there an elevator in your life? There's one in mine. Otis.

Every morning when I go to work I stand before Otis and summon him like royalty. "Stop here," I command with an imperial punch of my index finger. "Now."

Occasionally he does, but mostly he's a no-show. Otis is a public servant of sulky, sullen disposition. If Otis was a grade five student, his report card would read, "Does not take direction well."

Funny things, elevators. I am ancient enough to remember when the boxy beasts came with actual human operators. Perky widows or wizened gents, most often, complete with quasi-military uniforms and white gloves. They perched on wooden stools and operated a polished brass door handle and a bronze grill that fanned across the doorway between floors.

"Second floor," they would intone five thousand times a day. "Linens, woollens, notions, ladies lingerie, foundation garments." Or something like that, depending on the building their elevator graced.

The elevator operators are gone now, to that limboland that is home to the ghosts of telephone operators, stenographers and other sundry trades that have been subsumed by robots. Point is, riding an elevator used to be a humanizing experience. A chance to chew the fat with Old Eddie or Sweet Heloise, who you saw a couple or six times a day and whose life history you had a handle on. And who knew yours.

And now? Well, riding an elevator nowadays is . . . something else. A kind of suspended animation in which certain behavioural gestures are *de rigueur*.

You don't look directly at the other passengers. Rather you lift your eyes heavenwards to give the impression you are thinking great thoughts. The hands, if empty, are crossed over the nether regions. Talk—if any—is excruciatingly small.

"Some weather, eh?"

"Thank goodness it's Friday."

There are things one could do, of course, to enliven the thousands of elevator rides one is condemned to endure in one's lifetime. One could get on first on the ground floor, wait for the car to fill up, then burst into "The Maple Leaf Forever," briskly punching out the rhythm on the floor buttons.

One could, in a crowd of fellow travellers, open one's briefcase or purse, peer in and shout, "Getting enough air in there?"

One could, when arriving at one's floor, leap at the doors and attempt to claw them apart, then smile shamefaced when they open on their own.

One could do any or all of these things and more, but one won't, because one is Canadian. Canadians don't do such things.

Which may help explain a recent press release from a company called ENN.

ENN stands for—you may want to sit down for this—Elevator News Network. The name says it all. ENN is dedicated to electrifying the elevators of this country. So far they've hot-wired more than five hundred elevators in Toronto, Calgary and Vancouver.

Hot-wired for what? Why to carry newscasts, of course. Programming includes (I'm reading from the press release) "the latest local news, business, sports, market updates, ferry schedules, marine reports, ski conditions, weather and traffic information . . ."

ENN is sure this is going to be a big hit with elevator riders because, as an ENN spokesperson says, "It helps them pass the time and lets them catch up on current events."

Oh, yeah. The one thing I've been looking for to round out my life experience is up-to-the-minute details on earthquakes in Chile, bombs in Belfast, market upheavals in Tokyo and insurrection in Africa. Massacres, floods, plagues, plots and primaries during my commute from main to floor three.

Sorry, ENN. No offence, Otis.

But this is where I get off.

The Eureka File

"Chance makes a football of man's life."

Would you care to hazard a guess as to who said the above? Knute Rockne, maybe? Saddam Hussein? This week's head coach of the Ottawa Senators?

Wrong, wrong and wrong. The observation is more than twenty-five hundred years old. It comes from the writings of the ancient Greek dramatist and philosopher Sophocles.

A football. What a perfect analogy for the bounces—in bounds and out—that beset a body during its broken-field run down the gridiron of Life.

Life, when you think of it, is really a series of accidents all strung together like a necklace fashioned by a drunkard. We don't choose our parents. We don't select our place of birth. We don't elect to be left-handed, curly-haired, smart, dumb, tall or short. Those are all accidents that befall us.

As for the way our lives turn out, well, it all depends on how we play the "accidental" cards we were dealt.

Life isn't what happens to us. Life is what we do with the accidents that befall us.

It must be said that the vast majority of us play lousy poker. We take the accidents as they come, let them knock us down, and spend the rest of the game shrugging or blaming somebody else sitting at the table for our misfortune.

Some of us, but not all of us. Archimedes wasn't looking for a way to determine the volume of irregular objects when he sat down in a bathtub in Syracuse twenty-three hundred years ago. He was just looking for a nice hot soak, but when he saw how the water slopped over the top of the tub when he got in, a lightbulb flashed and Archimedes's Principle was born.

Isaac Newton, you may remember, had much the same experience under an apple tree. No doubt Newton was looking forward to a cozy nap in the orchard when that apple dropped. That accident led Newton to formulate what we know as the Law of Gravity.

There are many other happy accidents in the annals of science. Natural rubber isn't good for much in its natural state. It turns soft and sticky when it gets too warm, stiff and brittle when it cools off. Back in the early nineteenth century an American by the name of Charles Goodyear was fooling around with natural rubber, mixing it with various chemicals when he happened to spill a bit of it on a hot stove. To his surprise, the rubber didn't burn, but only charred slightly, as a piece of leather might.

Goodyear had accidentally discovered the process of vulcanizing rubber.

Little accidents sometimes yield grand results. Velcro? We owe its discovery to a walk in the woods that a Swiss inventor by the name of George de Mestral took about fifty years ago. When he got home, de Mestral noticed his pant legs were covered with burrs. Picking them off, he fell to wondering how such a little thing could stick so stubbornly. Under a microscope he discovered that the bristles of the burr ended in tiny hooks, invisible to the naked eye. Before long, de Mestral had found a way to duplicate the burr configuration in fabric, and Velcro fasteners were born.

Microwave ovens? In 1952, Dr. Percy Spencer was working

with radar when he noticed that a microwave leak had melted a chocolate bar in his pocket. He decided to try microwaving popcorn. Any couch potato knows how successful that experiment turned out.

One last happy accident of science. This one happened in the august kitchens of the Savoy Hotel in London around the turn of the century. A famous opera star was staying at the Savoy, and like many opera divas, she was striving mightily not to look like a battleship. The prima donna was dieting. Seriously. Living largely on a diet of toast and black tea.

She was such a star that the master chef was assigned to cook all her meals, even if she wanted only toast. But the prima donna came down early one morning, the master chef had not arrived and a culinary underling prepared her breakfast.

Disaster. The toast came out skinny and crustless. It looked like poached playing cards. As the Great Diva laid her divine choppers on the thin, emaciated slabs of bread, the master chef slunk out to her table ready to apologize. Before he could speak, the lady burst out, "Cesar, how clever of you. I have never eaten such lovely toast."

The lady's name was Nellie Melba.

And that's how the world got Melba toast.

A Bug in Your Ear

The *Globe and Mail* headline blared the news: "Cellphones Safe, U.S. Study Finds." Scientists have determined that cellular telephones don't give users brain cancer after all.

My first reaction was: damn! I'd been pulling for the brain cancer option. Anything that might slacken the death grip of that single most invasive and obnoxious morsel of modern technology.

I know, I know. The cellphone is a godsend for marooned mountaineers, stranded motorists and anybody who can't come up with two bits for a pay phone. But when did it become mandatory for everybody with an opposable thumb to pack one? The damn things are everywhere. For a while I thought the streets of my town were home to a mass epidemic of earaches. People were all walking around with one hand jammed to the side of their head. Then I realized they were on cellphones.

People can't seem to just walk or sit in contemplative silence anymore. They have to call somebody. Right now. And it's only going to get worse.

Check the local schoolyard. Little prepubertal schoolkids cling to their cellphones as if they were locks of Britney Spears's hair. As a matter of fact, that relates to the latest application for the cellphone; it's become a pop concert accessory. Kids take their Nokias and Motorolas to performances by their favourite stars, and in the middle of the show they whip them out, dial up a friend and wave the cellphone at the stage so that their non-ticket-buying friends can experience the next best thing to being there.

Pretty spooky, but if a couple of Frankenstein wannabes over in the UK have their way, Cellphoneworld will soon become even spookier.

Two researchers affiliated with the European partner of the Massachusetts Institute of Technology have come up with what they call the audio tooth implant, also known as the molar mobile or the telephone tooth. It is a tiny receiver that can be implanted in one of your back teeth. The device allows the patient, hereafter referred to as the schmuck, to receive phone calls, listen to music, even connect to sound sites on the Internet, directly on a back molar which then transmits the audio signal through the jawbone to the inner ear.

The inventors aren't just targeting brain-dead, headbanger teenagers. They reckon the device will be popular with investors and brokers, not to mention sports fanatics desperate to follow the play-by-play of their favourite teams around the clock.

The brainiacs behind the telephone tooth haven't figured out a way to make outgoing calls, but, given the breakneck pace of technology—cellphone wasn't even a recognized noun twenty years ago—it's only a matter of time.

I take solace in the fact that the term cellphone rage is growing even faster than cellphone mania. Innocent bystanders are finally standing up and yelling back at the ignorant yackers and jabberers in our midst. A woman on a BC ferry was recently yapping into her cellphone in the middle of the lounge when a fellow passenger said in a loud voice, "Madame, I think I speak for the other passengers here when I say we don't care to hear about the gossip from your office, so please finish your call or take it out on the deck."

Cellphone resentment in Toronto runs even higher. Doctors at Toronto General report treating mobile phone talkers for black eyes and even in one case, a cracked rib, all results of cellphone rage.

The actor Lawrence Fishburne stopped in mid-performance during a Broadway play last year, fixed a member of the audience with a glare and bellowed, "Will you turn off that (expletive) phone, please?"

He got a standing ovation.

Speaking of standing, that's what I was doing in a highway restroom recently, minding my own business when a voice floated over the wall of the cubicle next to me.

"Hi," it said.

"Hi," I answered uncertainly.

There was a pause, then the voice said, "What are you doing?"

"Well," I stammered, "I'm just making a pit stop, I'm travelling west on the highway, just like you are, I guess."

There was an even longer silence. Then the voice said, "Look, honey, I'll call you back. Some idiot at the urinals is answering every question I ask you."

Cellphones. I hate 'em.

The New Rattletrap SE 4.0

They say familiarity breeds contempt. I don't know about contempt, but I'm dead sure that having certain things around can make you take them for granted.

Take the jalopy. Also known as the set of wheels, bucket of bolts, puddle-jumper, heap, crate, chug-along, tin lizzie, rattletrap, junker or beater. Now there's something we take for granted.

Every day most of us commit our bodies to contraptions with names like Chrysler, Chevrolet, Pontiac or Cadillac stamped on their noses. More exotic travellers sit in vehicles that carry monikers such as Audi, Lexus, SAAB, BMW or Fiat.

But how many of us know what those names mean?

Well, last things first. Fiat is an acronym, formed by the first letters of Fabrica Italiana Automobili Torino. Same story for the German BMW, which stands for Bavarian Motor Works. SAAB is almost an acronym; it stands for Swedish Airplane Inc.

Don't ask me where the airplane fits into it. SAABs are fast, but they're not that fast.

As for the name Audi, that's a little cleverer. August Horch was a German car maker who, for obscure legal reasons, was prohibited by law from putting his name on any automobiles he created. Trouble is, he had this hot new car and enough ego to want to see his name on the hood.

What to do? Well, in German, *horch* means to hear or to listen. In Latin, the verb for to hear or listen is *audire*. August Horch named his new car Audi and put one over on the German lawyers. At least the non-Latin-speaking ones.

As for Lexus, well, it sounds Latin, but it isn't. Lexus is a totally made up word coined to describe Toyota's top of the line car. They thought Lexus sounded, well . . . luxurious.

So much for the hothouse plants of the automotive world. What about the more prosaic, home-bred varieties?

You may not think of a Chrysler as prosaic, but its origins are. It comes from Walter Percy Chrysler, who got his start as a sweeper in a railway roundhouse.

The Cadillac is named after a seventeenth-century French fur trader, Antoine de la Mothe Cadillac, who made Motor City possible by erecting a trading post at what would become Detroit. Pontiac was an eighteenth-century Indian chief who laid siege to Detroit, which was held by the English at the time. Chevys take their name from Louis Chevrolet, a guy who raced cars back when going ninety kilometres an hour was tantamount to breaking the sound barrier.

Then of course there's Henry Ford, the father of the mass-produced automobile and perhaps the only carmaker whose persona remains as firmly identified as his product.

Well, there was one other, almost. An Austrian who backed the production of a curious little German mechanical critter back in the thirties. His car was homely, slow and rather dinky in comparison to the land yachts that North American car manufacturers were turning out.

This guy wanted to call his car the K of F Wagon, standing for *Kraft Durch Freude*, which means strength through joy. Saner heads prevailed and the car hit the market as the Volkswagen. *Kraft Durch Freude* is a clumsy name for anything and a bad marketing idea.

But then that Austrian guy had a lot of bad ideas. His name was Adolf Hitler.

Car names—they're fascinating. Honda, Toyota and Hyundai sound almost impossibly exotic. In fact they are simply named after the guys who first manufactured them.

Datsun? Well, I can't vouch for it, but my friend Ernie the Barfly down at Moe's Tap Room claims he knows where the name comes from.

"A bunch of Detroit carmakers went to Japan a few years back," says Ernie. "They were looking for a Japanese company that could turn out a new economy car for them. They finally settled on an automotive plant on the outskirts of Yokohama. They were sold when the plant manager promised them ultra-speedy delivery.

"They asked him how soon they could get their first consignment of the new cars.

"'Three weeks,' the plant manager replied.

"The Detroit guys were dumbfounded," says Ernie. "Their jaws dropped, their eyes bugged out, they looked at the plant manager and said all together . . .

"'Datsun?'"

You Must Remember Disk

Nothing like the Death of a Giant to kick the slats out of the media's adjective corral. Reporters love Big Deaths. When a Trudeau topples or a Queen Mum passes the papers are instantly awash in ink. The TV talking heads wag in stately two-four time; the radio announcers drone on at great lugubrious length. Solemn editorials are penned; paeans from anguished readers speckle the letters to the editor page.

Quite a chasm between the funereal gushes the great receive and the seven or eight line obligatory obit you and I will rate when we finally kick—but that's okay. We won't be around to read it anyway.

But there's a group of humans who really get shafted when they shuffle off the mortal coil. I mean the folks who deserve a big tribute but don't get it. Sure, the artists who write great books, compose timeless music and paint masterpieces deserve praise at their passing. Likewise for the geniuses who invented penicillin and smashed the atom. But what about the others? What about, for instance, Ed Headrick?

You bet Ed Headrick! Born 1904, died a while back—and hardly a peep in the press about it. Oh, he got a reasonably warm couple of paragraphs in the *Globe and Mail*. They mentioned how Ed was a World War II vet and how he liked to play the xylophone, but this was buried in the back pages. For my money,

Ed's death should have been a front page, stop the press, banner headlined feature story.

Because Ed Headrick invented the Frisbee.

Well, not so much invented, as refined it. College kids had been flinging paint can lids, plastic tops and various and sundry disks since the 1950s. (As a matter of fact, the very name Frisbee comes from an old pie tin that was manufactured by the Frisbie Baking Company.) It was a lot of fun but you were never quite sure what the disk was going to do once you launched it. A company named Wham-O came up with a patented plastic toy it called the Flying Saucer. It performed somewhat better and it looked a lot like a Frisbee except for one tiny feature: the top was as smooth as a baby's bottom.

That's where Ed Headrick came in. Back in 1964, Ed discovered that adding a series of tiny ridges in the form of concentric circles across the top of the toy stabilized the flight path. Suddenly it didn't wobble any more. Hey, presto! The Frisbee was born.

The funny thing about Ed is he really loved his Frisbee. He went on to invent Disk Golf, in which players eschew their irons and woods in favour of Frisbees, which they fling at targets laid out like the holes at a golf course. Ed Headrick not only invented the game, he excelled at it. He was World Champion. Twice.

Did he take the game and the toy seriously? You bet. He liked to call his fellow addicts Frisbyterians. When he reached his nineties, Ed Headrick sort of wrote his own obituary. He requested that his ashes be moulded into a limited number of "memorial flying disks" to be distributed to a select group of family and friends.

Frisbyterians all, naturally.

But what a way to go! Knowing that on any given sunny afternoon, chances are there's a part of you out there in a park or on a back lawn sailing through the air from the fingertips of one friend to the fingertips of another.

That's better than a five-page obituary.

Better too, than leaving those last-minute arrangements to

someone else who turns out to be not quite as sympathetic as one would like. I'm reminded of the telephone call to the obituary department of a newspaper in Toronto some years ago.

"How much does it cost to have an obituary printed?" asked the caller.

"It's five dollars a word, ma'am," said the newspaper guy.

"Fine," said the woman. "Got a pencil?"

"Yes, ma'am."

"Got some paper?"

"Yes, ma'am."

"Then take this down: MacTavish . . . dead."

The reporter waited for the woman to go on. Nothing.

"That's it?" he asked.

"That's it," said the woman.

"I'm sorry, I should have told you, ma'am, there's a five-word minimum."

"Yes, you should have, young man," snapped the woman. "All right, let me think . . . Got a pencil?

"Yes, ma'am."

"Got some paper?"

"Yes, ma'am."

"Then take this down: MacTavish dead. Bagpipes for sale."

Beam Me Up, Alexander

In 1793 Scottish fur trader and explorer Alexander Mackenzie travelled overland from Lake Athabaska to the Pacific Ocean, north of Vancouver Island. He did it by raft, canoe and on foot and it took him the best part of a spring, summer and fall.

In 1952 my brother-in-law Roy travelled from Toronto to the Pacific coast. He did it behind the wheel of a '47 Buick, driving pretty much night and day. It took him a week.

Last month I made the same journey, Toronto to Vancouver. I did it in an Air Canada 727. It took me . . . about one afternoon, if you don't count the wait at the luggage carousel.

When Mackenzie made his trek, he faced blackflies, grizzlies, hostile Indians, starvation, gumbo, frost, hail and thunderstorms.

My brother-in-law had to worry about black ice, potholes, running out of gas and falling asleep at the wheel. Had to go to a doctor to get his eyes closed when he got to Vancouver.

Last week my travel perils included a seat that wouldn't recline quite properly, a dinner of virtual chicken and ice cold cutlery. (Where do they store that stuff?)

As travellers, we've come a long way, *bambino*, and it hasn't necessarily made us more resourceful or admirable. Relatively speaking, air travel today is not all that far from the *Starship*

Enterprise and those molecular transporters Captain Kirk and the lads use to boldly go where no man has gone before.

And that is quite a beam-up, Scotty. For most of mankind's tenancy on this planet, serious travel has customarily involved hardship, exertion, a certain potential for danger and quite an outlay of time. But now? Now travel is just a matter of delivering yourself up to the nearest airport, safety-belting yourself into an oversized aluminum cigar tube and then thumbing through last week's *Maclean's* while the cigar tube delivers you to another nearly identical airport.

It's safe. It's convenient, and it's dizzyingly fast compared to the ploddings of an eighteenth-century explorer or even a '47 Buick.

But in terms of zest, it's flatter than week-old ginger ale. Antiheroic. A glorified elevator ride, really. Textureless, much like the virtual chicken dinner they serve.

Alexander Mackenzie walked, paddled and poled every foot of his journey when he crossed the Rockies in 1793. My brother-in-law was only marginally insulated from the land by the tires and the windshield of his Buick when he did it a century and a half later.

And me? On Flight 998 Toronto to Vancouver?

I flew at ten thousand metres. I was in my shirt sleeves, sipping a glass of wine, with my shoes off. Even on a clear day I couldn't have seen a '47 Buick down on the ground, much less a solitary Scottish fur trader plodding along.

I did have one small advantage over Mackenzie and my brother-in-law. I could actually see the peak of Mount Robson, the highest mountain in the Canadian Rockies out my window at eye level as my plane flew by it, just north of Jasper.

Well, I could have seen it . . . but the flight attendant asked me if I wouldn't mind lowering my window shade.

The inflight movie was playing. They wanted to keep it nice and dark so that we passengers could enjoy *Chicken Run.*